HEART BURN

A SIX-WEEK STUDY OF THE PSALMS

HEART BURN

Blazing Hot Worship

featuring the music of

Spooky Tuesday, One Eighty, Havalina Rail Co., Soul-Junk and Sierra Hart

Rick Bundschuh

EMPOWERED™ Youth Products
Standard Publishing
Cincinnati, Ohio

Cover and inside design by Dina Sorn
Edited by Dale Reeves and Leslie Durden

Standard Publishing, Cincinnati, Ohio.
A division of Standex International Corporation.

Special thanks to Jackson Rubio and BEC Recordings.

06   05   04   03   02   01   00   99
5   4   3   2   1

ISBN: 0-7847-0930-0

Contents

Introduction

It starts as a spark of longing or a flash of insight. Allowing the breath of the Holy Spirit to gently blow, it fans into flame. It is a heart on fire for God . . . divine heartburn.

The small grind of everyday life can have a cooling effect on our spiritual life. Over the centuries, seekers of God have found that making the effort to worship their Creator has rekindled the divine blaze, stoked the fire of spiritual service and for some, ignited their hearts for the first time.

Welcome to six fire-starting sessions on worship from the book of Psalms . . . the songbook (or overhead collection) of God's people. This six-week course of the Psalms is designed to set your students ablaze by exploring the breadth and depth of God-centered worship. The match and lighter fluid to make this happen are hands-on biblical discovery and participation in worship using red-hot modern Christian music.

WE ARE CREATED TO WORSHIP

Human beings are designed to worship God. The need, the craving and thirst to enter into the experience of worship is interwoven into our souls. The longing for worship often lays dormant in those who are far from God, but once awakened, the encounter that takes place by communing with the Living Creator becomes refreshing, comfortable and natural. The warm coals produced by an act of devotion to God can sustain us through a winter of doubt and trouble.

Worship is not merely an experience that takes place within the church or during a specifically designed hour set aside for the purpose. Worship is also the actions of our lives, the priorities of our hearts and the dedication of our endeavors. We can live our lives as a daily act of worship or we can, even in little ways, deny God and direct our worship towards temporal idols.

MUSIC AND WORSHIP

Music has historically been used as a vehicle for worship. The ancient Hebrews celebrated and praised God in chants and song, most with musical accompaniment. While the tunes they used have been lost, their words have been retained in the book of Psalms. The early church sang hymns of original composition and choruses from the Psalms as they gathered in the pre-workday dawn of Sunday morning. Each century those of the faith have mingled their own musical styles and traditions with the timeless ideas and words of the Bible to give glory to God.

This course uses modern music to communicate ideas about worship or to actually lead students into a worship experience. Utilizing either words directly from the Psalms or those that clearly reflect the concepts found in Scripture, the songs are woven into each session but can also become part of the group's repertoire of regularly used worship tunes.

The power and energy of worship is an irresistible flame, igniting believers and unbelievers with the fire that comes from the heart of God. As your students join in to revere and adore their Creator, they will find themselves humbled, inspired, purified and strengthened.

PARTS AND PIECES OF HEARTBURN

Each session in this book is divided into three sections: **Striking the Match, Fanning the Flame** and **Divine HeartBurn.** Each of these sections contains more than one option or activity for you to use, depending on available resources and the needs of your students. As you prepare to teach, tailor the lesson to fit your group's learning style and focus on the topic your students most need to learn about. Customize as you see fit.

Striking the Match gets your students connected to the direction the Scripture will lead them in for each session. Choose whichever option you think would work best with your students.

Fanning the Flame is the heart of the lesson, where the Bible is cracked open, the theme is discussed and dissected. Choose from the various interactive options to involve your students in a meaningful study of God's Word.

Lastly, **Divine HeartBurn** offers students something they can apply to their lives individually. These activities are usually of a private and personal nature, something between the student and God. Use care when asking students to share their thoughts and decisions in these areas.

As this course has a heavy utilization of Christian music, you will notice in the margins all kinds of ideas that you can use to add dimension and spice to your session. Some of these involve not only music but other kinds of media as well. If you decide to use any of the media or song clips that come from secular sources (there are a few), keep in mind that these clips are not an endorsement for the whole performance, idea or artists involved. These clips are merely a teaching tool that grabs a usable portion to make help make a point. Standard Publishing does not necessarily endorse the entire contents of a particular movie or album.

The Psalms are imbedded with meaning that is just as powerful in summoning God's people to worship as it was thousands of years ago. It is in worship that we find both his strength and our security. It is in worship that our hearts and lives ignite.

How to Use the Music

This course has the exciting feature of a free CD containing six hot *original* praise and worship songs by both established and up-and-coming Christian artists. In addition, there are chord sheets for those in your group who would like to learn and lead these songs, as well as lyric sheets for use as overheads in singing along. Plus, you have the artists' permission to use songs with your youth group anytime you like!

The music included can be used in a number of ways:

1 As part of the lesson.

Each session has a selection written into it. You may choose to use this option or choose an alternative. If you choose to use the song as part of the session, you may teach it to your youth group at that point in the presentation, listen to it off the CD, sing along with the recording or merely pass out the lyric sheet.

2 As part of your praise and worship time.

Any or all of the songs included can be learned fairly easily and incorporated into the material you are already using. If you have students who are talented with instruments, you may want to hand them the CD and chord sheets and let them come up with their own version of the songs. A student-led praise and worship group gives both ownership and excitement.

3 As pure enjoyment.

Teenagers love music and while the songs on this CD are worship tunes, they also rock! Your students will enjoy these songs anytime!

4 As encouragement.

Many students listen to lots of lousy stuff. All of the bands on this CD also have other material available in Christian bookstores. Their biographies are included in this book. Whet your students' appetite for great Christian music by introducing them to these artists.

Spooky Tuesday

Spooky Tuesday was founded in 1994 on the island of Kauai, Hawaii, while all of the band members were still in high school. The sound of this young quartet of committed Christians has been described as "pop/folk/neo-alterna-rock & roll." Other tags that have been put on them include "that alterna-pop-rock-folk-acoustic sound that prevents them from being pigeonholed," and "progressive modern rock with lyrics that reflect on the realities facing young people entering the next century."

Pulling their name from dialogue in an afternoon "creature feature," the band was formed to compete in a high school talent contest, which they lost to an Elvis impersonator. The loss provided the impetus to press forward. The band entered the charts for the first time in 1996 with their debut, *It'll Never Fly Orville,* while they were all high school students. Their sophomore release, *Happy Dissonance,* in 1997 indicated a more complex direction the band was starting to take, culminating in their 1999 release, *The Trouble We Make,* with Jackson Rubio Recordings.

Never a band to back away from tough issues, some of their work tackles problems that today's teens are very familiar with: drug use, incest, suicide and self-centeredness, all presented with a definitive Christian perspective. They make no apologies for their faith and even their darkest songs point to the hope found in Jesus Christ.

More than just music, Spooky Tuesday is all about ministry, as evidenced by their mission statement: "We desire that young men and women be pointed to Christ through the gifts, talents and opportunities that he has given us. We desire to be a service to both the local church and the community of believers throughout the world." The band has made themselves accountable to the elders of their local church in Kauai.

Spooky Tuesday is

Justin "Pepe" Bundschuh
bass, graphic design

Andrew Neuman
guitars, lead vocals

Jessica Treskon
lead guitars, vocals

Kevin Penner
drums, web designer

Web site:
www.jesusfreak.com/spookytuesday/

Management:

Rick Bundschuh
(888) 742-5428
fax: (808) 332-5916
e-mail: pastor@aloha.net

"The realization of grace in my life is what draws me towards worshiping God—when I realize how small I am in relationship to God, and then I realize his might. His sacrifice through Jesus compels me to worship." —Andrew Neuman

One Eighty

One Eighty is

Kim Tennberg
vocals, trumpet

Madelyn Mendoza
vocals, percussion

Chris Tennberg
rhythm guitar

Jerry Elekes
lead guitar

Dave DesArmier
bass

Jamin Boggs
drums

John Anderson
saxophone

Josh Brisby
trombone

Publicity:

teresa@toothandnail.com
fax: (206) 382-1131

booking:
Chris: (760) 724-1497

Begun in May of 1995, One Eighty was the vision of a group of college students who wanted to contribute to what was then the early groundbreaking advances in female-fronted ska-punk. Influenced by bands like Dance Hall Crashers, Dakoda Motor Co and MxPx, One Eighty quickly conquered the local scene with their customized energetic sound and the catchy one-two vocal punch of Kim Tennberg and Madelyn Mendoza.

The songs of One Eighty are distinguished by their undeniably catchy melodies and harmonies, but the band also sets itself apart with a positive message inspired by the band members' faith in God. Guitarist Chris Tennberg, who recently earned his religion degree from Southern California College, explains this higher influence: "We sing about events that happen in everyday life, but we reflect on these events from a Christian point of view. We consider a situation and ask ourselves, 'How would a Christian handle this?'" This approach gives the listener a positive message, but the down-to-earth perspective draws listeners in rather than alienating people the way some message-filled songs can.

Produced by Gene Eugene, One Eighty's debut album, *Crackerjack*, has the hooks loved by radio, and the energy loved by kids. In the words of *7Ball* magazine, this group's style "unites the best of ska, punk, surf, skate, swing and every other genre which makes up the adrenalized culture of beach music."

"At times, the modern mentality in worship is too caught up in the performance, entertainment appeal to the congregation rather than a more humble, reverent approach. The eye-catching display of the dramatic vocalists, array of instruments, yelling preacher, and the overextended, long-and-drawn-out song can often become a big distraction from the sole purpose of focusing on God."—Kim Tennberg

Soul-Junk

Soul-Junk, who plays rock with a touch of groove sprinkled throughout, began in 1993 when Trumans Water guitarist and vocalist Glen "Galaxy" Galloway felt the call to compress his opuses into spirituals. Galloway recorded Soul-Junk's first two records single-handedly. By the end of 1994, Soul-Junk had filled out to band status with Brian Cantrell on drums and Ron Easterbrooks also on guitar. This lineup did the third and fourth records, *1952* and *1953*. By this point they had added Glen's brother Jon on bass. Concerning *1953*, one reviewer said, "The Junk have blessed us with religiously soulful, melodic tunes, yet still manage to remain an underground favorite."

Since *1954* was a bonus album snuck in on the last CD, the newest release from Soul-Junk is *1955*. Soul-Junk advocates omnidirectional sound, which recognizes all forms of music (discovered and undiscovered, beat-driven and ambient), as if surrounding all listeners lying on a 360-degree spectrum. Rather than fixate on any one point in the spectrum, they beam in from any and all points, featuring garage-flavored rock, jump-up jungle, kiss-the-sky improvisation, new-school hip hop and resonant drone/sound apocalypses. This indie rock group has been featured in *Details*, *Alternative Press*, *Magnet* and *Etch* magazines.

The fact that they quote the Bible in almost every song accounts for the unusual power of their lyrics. In fact, it has been estimated that eighty percent of their lyrics are taken directly from God's Word. One reviewer has described their music as "Biblical passages and other food for the soul arranged in an inimitable, shambling, rock-funk-folk idiom." Perhaps the best way to describe this band is in their own words, spoken in the midst of a concert: "Consider the possibility tonight that what you've rejected is not God; it's man's attempts to play God. Please allow us to worship the one we call our God openly in front of you tonight. We ask that our Jesus would demonstrate the inner truth of these words—that God is a Spirit and we worship him in spirit and truth. Let us provide a soundtrack of reconciliation for you. We sing peace to those far and near in the name of Jesus."

Soul-Junk is

Glen Galloway
guitars, vocals

Jon Galloway
bass

Ron Easterbrooks
guitar

Booking:

(415) 826-0647
www.jacksonrubio.com

"Music is one of the few things we haven't yet learned to totally intellectualize. It's one of the only spiritual experiences western culture 'allows,' and even encourages. I don't know exactly how it works, but music can usually get past my usual thought patterns to intense feelings inside me. That's why I think it's so important to be chasing down new ways to worship God with music. Satan is constantly coming up with new ways to get into our thoughts to pull us away from God. So, if music can help pull us into God, then let's go hard in that direction."
—Glen Galloway

Havalina Rail Co.

Havalina Rail Co. is

Matt Wignall
guitar, vocals

Orlando Greenhill
upright bass, electric bass

Jeff Suri
drums, vocals

Lori Suri
vocals, washboard

Mark Cole
percussion, bells

Erick Diego Nieto de Ecuador
violin

Booking:

matt@jacksonrubio.com
(562) 425-5610
fax: (562) 425-0032

Since its inception in 1992, Havalina Rail Co. has had a quirky flare for the mysterious. On the first and second records, they pushed traditional styles of American music to new places in an attempt to redefine what music is. During the songwriting process for its third album, Havalina came across the romantic images of eastern Europe through literature and sound, and embarked on the musical journey, "Russian Lullabies," to define its personal impressions of eastern Europe.

The music is described by this six-piece band from Long Beach, California, as trying to do what Stravinsky once did with jazz. Without ever hearing jazz, he attempted to compose pieces based on what he had read about it. The music ended up nothing like jazz. Similarly, Havalina Rail Co.'s impressions of eastern Europe are sketches of sounds and melodies, a melting pot of the pop music they were raised on, and the art music they have grown to love.

Havalina has been involved in the Christian music industry since 1993, when they recorded their first album with Tooth & Nail Records. The philosophy behind Havalina's music is rooted directly in its Christianity. They believe, as expressed by frontman Matt Wignall, that "Christianity is a worldview that affects all of life, not just our Sunday morning church life." Based on this belief, they strive for their art to be experimental, entertaining and fun. Havalina Rail Co. believes that exercising its creativity can be a form of worshiping God and showing a small part of his character to the world.

> *"I believe that we can worship God in anything that we do—surfing, playing music, etc. It is an attitude toward all of life that makes doing these things an act of worship, since God is the God of all life. We can see elements of his grace touching all parts of our lives."—Matt Wignall*

Sierra Hart

Sierra Hart grew up in Southern California and at an early age found her niche in singing folk-influenced worship music. She learned how to sing and play guitar when she was quite young, and spent her high school years singing worship music in her church's band. During those years, she began writing her own songs, most of which are stories derived from her life and the lives of friends around her who were struggling through early stages of Christianity.

Booking:

(831) 689-5386
sierrahart@chickmail.com

In between her studies at the University of California in Santa Cruz, Sierra Hart has been able to share the songs God has inspired in her heart at youth outreach events, coffeehouses and worship times in churches. On her latest release entitled *Sojourner*, Sierra's songs are witty and rich in theological content—and they demonstrate her willingness to tackle her hopes, fears and frustrations with the world today. Most of all, her music carries the hope that is found in knowing that everything is in God's hands. Sierra's heart is revealed in her own words: "I do not pretend to be a super Christian or to have this high calling mastered. I only thank Jesus Christ my Lord for loving me despite my failures and struggles and for giving me a brand-new chance every morning to become a clearer reflection of his beauty and tenderness and grace."

"When life gets too complicated, and problems seem impossible to solve, I need to remember that all things are possible with God. I realize that it is not in my power to solve problems and fix relationships; it is in God's power and ability. Worship reminds me that it is God's desire to take care of me, so I don't have to try to make everything work the way I think it should. Worship gives us strength and renewed hope and love for God. It gives us renewed love for others, and a spirit of forgiveness. Worship humbles us. It takes the focus off us and puts it onto Jesus, and our desperate need for Him. Worship restores balance to our life, because it makes us turn our heart and mind over to God, which is exactly where they belong."—Sierra Hart

A Homesick Heart

INTRODUCTION

Some places just feel good. They are comfortable because they allow us to drop the pretenses that often layer our public lives and, for good or for bad, be ourselves. We usually call this place "home."

Of course, our home is not just where we can trot around in a ratty shirt and worn shorts; it is the place where caring, tenderness and nurture take place. It is the lodging of those who love us in spite of having seen us when we are at our very worst and most selfish.

A gift that God gives to every Christian is the dawning idea that the incredible sense of well-being, love, peace and satisfaction we find so tantalizing is found in the presence of God only. The writer of Psalm 84 likens it to a physical location—the house of the Lord.

C. S. Lewis once commented about the writers of the Psalms: "These poets knew far less reason than we for loving God. They did not know that He offered them eternal joy: still less that He would die to win it for them. Yet they express a longing for Him, for His mere presence, which comes only to the best Christians or to Christians in their best moments. They long to live in the Temple so that they may constantly see 'the fair beauty of the Lord'" (*Reflections on the Psalms*).

While no doubt this psalmist had the Hebrew temple in mind as he penned the words, the concept works in the abstract sense as well.

The path to God's presence is most often found in worship. In our yearning for him, we are met and escorted into a foretaste of the cleanliness, joy, comfort and peace that awaits us in eternity.

This session is designed to help students see that by the very act of worship they are able to move on to that pilgrimage towards a spiritual "home" where every desire is met and every restless heart is stilled—a place where God himself resides. A place that even now when we worship, sure feels good.

STRIKING THE MATCH

① *There's No Place Like Home*

Start your meeting by showing a clip from the classic movie *The Wizard of Oz*. Locate the place in the movie where Dorothy is homesick and fearful of not getting back to Auntie Em and the gang (about 135 minutes into the film) or where she clicks her ruby slippers (about

---

LESSON TEXT
Psalm 84; Luke 15:11-32

LESSON FOCUS
Being in God's presence is the only place to find true joy and satisfaction.

LESSON GOALS
As a result of participating in this lesson, students will:
- Explore the biblical symbolism of being in God's presence.
- Discuss the things that cause us to stray from our Father.
- Offer an act of worship in song as a way to enter God's presence.

Materials needed:
Video/DVD player; TV or projector; video of *The Wizard of Oz*

140 minutes into the movie) and gets taken back to Kansas.

Introduce the film clip by saying something like this, **"One of the things that makes a movie a classic is the ability of the screenwriters to tap into common but powerful human emotions in a clever way. A classic example of this can be found in the movie clip we are about to take a look at. See if you can figure out the heart chord that is being struck by this bit of filmmaking genius."**

After viewing the film clip, give your students a chance to comment on what they think was the universal human emotion touched in that part of the film. Introduce the central point of the session by saying something like this: **"The idea that 'home' is where real safety and comfort is found is true not only on a human dimension but it is absolutely true on a spiritual dimension. The human heart is designed not only to find comfort and peace in familiar surroundings but to find it ultimately in the presence of God. The writers of the choruses we call Psalms understood this. Today we are going to take a look at a poetic example which compares this desire to be with God to a pilgrimage to God's home."**

② I Can Hardly Wait to Get Back to . . .

Invite your students to take a look at the student sheet on page 19 of this book. Ask them to fill in the things that they most appreciate about going home after a long trip in the order of priority to them.

After a few minutes, ask your students to share what they have written. Discuss why, for most people, "there's no place like home."

Direct your students to the subject of this session by saying, **"The Bible gives us a similar example of the peace and joy that each human is looking for but not finding in life. The Psalm we are going to look at today suggests that the place where we find real contentment, acceptance and joy is in the presence of God. The writer uses the analogy of a princely home to suggest where we want to be moving toward if we want to enjoy our hearts' true home."**

FANNING THE FLAME

① The Illustrated Psalm

Hand out sheets of paper, pencils and markers to your students. Ask them to form groups of three to five, perhaps grouping them by their top selections of favorite things about home, from among the top five choices from previous activity, if used. Then assign each group all or a portion of Psalm 84 (you could include the Parable of the Prodigal Son found in Luke 15:11-32 as well if you have enough groups) to illustrate visually. Comment, **"Please take a look at the passage of Scripture I have assigned to you and see if you can communicate the ideas in it in a visual fashion. Use symbols and drawings and as few words as possible. Number your illustrations so that we can post them on the wall to see if we can make sense of your ideas."**

Give your groups enough time to work and then post their efforts around the room for everyone to see. Discuss what they have created and the meaning behind their drawings.

Tell students: **"Jesus picked up on the theme of Psalm 84 —The dwelling place of God being the place of joy and safety for a believer—with the Parable of the Prodigal Son."** Initiate a discussion about the way Christians can find themselves in an uncomfortable place, far from the heart and love of their Father by asking questions such as these:

- **How do Christians find themselves in "pigpen living" or straying far from home?**
- **In what way does worship help bring a person home to God?**
- **How does getting back home with God make you feel?**

② *Symbols of a Journey Home*

Ask your students to read Psalm 84 and then work individually or in pairs to complete the "Finding the Way" section of the student sheet on page 20. Discuss with your group the powerful meanings behind the symbolic ideas presented in the Psalms.

Ask your students to read Luke 15:11-32 and to be prepared to retell in words, pictures or drama a modern version of the parable. Break into appropriately sized groups, provide any necessary materials and give your students some time to work on their presentations.

After your students have shared their efforts with the rest of the group, discuss the idea that entering into true worship with God is like coming home.

Ask questions such as these:

- **In the journey of a Christian, how does regular worship help us not to stray as far off God's path?**
- **What emotions and feelings come about as a result of entering into praise and worship?**
- **For the writer of the Psalms, going to the temple was entering in the realm of God's presence. How or where do you go to enter into God's presence?**
- **For the prodigal son, coming back home was an occasion for a party. In what way can worship be a celebration or party commemorating God's forgiveness and love for us?**

DIVINE HEARTBURN

① *Everything I Want (Is in You)*

Begin this activity by saying, **"Suppose you were suddenly made aware of God's physical presence, like Moses was when he saw the burning bush. How would you feel? Which of these words best expresses how it might be for you to find yourself in a spiritual encounter like that: Fearful? ashamed? joyful? at peace? insignificant? terrified? shocked? confused? guilty? cautious? overwhelmed? embarrassed? excited?"**

Materials needed:
Reproducible student sheet on page 20 of this book; writing utensils; various sizes of paper; markers; Bibles

Materials needed:
CD player; CD packaged with this book; overhead or reproducible lyric sheet on page 77 of this book

Materials needed:
CD player; CD packaged with this book; reproducible lyric sheet on page 77 of this book; writing utensils

Materials needed:
Reproducible student sheets on pages 55-69 of this book

After reading the list of possible responses, allow several students to share their emotional reactions to such an event.

Make sure that everyone has the words to Spooky Tuesday's praise and worship song "Everything I Want (Is in You)" from page 77 of this book. After you have listened to the song, throw out these questions for consideration by the group:

- **Think of some things that you want out of life. Can any of those things fulfill a person for long?**
- **Which commandments did Jesus say were the greatest? How do they give peace and satisfaction to our lives?**
- **If God were really what we desire most, how would we live and act?**

Sing the song together as a closing act of worship.

② Am I Heading Toward Home?

Put the CD of Spooky Tuesday's "Everything I Want (Is in You)" on the player and make sure each student has a copy of the words. As the song is playing several times in the background, ask students to look at the words of the song and to underline statements in the lyrics that express their attitude towards God.

EVERY DAY IN WORSHIP

Distribute copies of the reproducible sheets on pages 55-69 to your students. Explain how they are to cut apart the slips of paper and read one Psalm a day over the course of this study. Then, each week check in with them to see how they are doing.

I can Hardly wait to get Back to . . .

Circle the things that you can hardly wait to get back to after you've been away from home on a long grueling trip or camping expedition. Put a star by the ones that you think would be on the top five of your list if you were to come home from a trip like that today.

my own bed	my mom's home cooking	my dog, cat, iguana or gerbil
my friends	my boyfriend or girlfriend	my music collection
my shower	my neighborhood	my brothers or sisters
my sports	my hobbies	a different set of my clothes
my car	my TV or video games	my sofa or easy chair
my church	my parents	my musical instruments
my room	my computer	my school

"Knowing that I will find peace in his Spirit draws me to God; it feels so good just to completely dedicate some time to the Lord."—Jessica Penner of Spooky Tuesday

Finding the Way

Psalm 84:1-12
For the director of music. According to *gittith*. Of the Sons of Korah. A psalm.

"How lovely is your dwelling place, O LORD Almighty!
My soul yearns, even faints, for the courts of the LORD;
my heart and my flesh cry out for the living God.
Even the sparrow has found a home, and the swallow a nest for herself, where she may have her young—a
place near your altar, O LORD Almighty, my King and my God.
Blessed are those who dwell in your house; they are ever praising you.
Selah
Blessed are those whose strength is in you, who have set their hearts on pilgrimage.
As they pass through the Valley of Baca, they make it a place of springs; the autumn rains also cover it with
pools.
They go from strength to strength, till each appears before God in Zion.
Hear my prayer, O LORD God Almighty; listen to me, O God of Jacob.
Selah
Look upon our shield, O God; look with favor on your anointed one.
Better is one day in your courts than a thousand elsewhere; I would rather be a doorkeeper in the house of my
God than dwell in the tents of the wicked.
For the LORD God is a sun and shield; the LORD bestows favor and honor; no good thing does he withhold from
those whose walk is blameless.
O LORD Almighty, blessed is the man who trusts in you."

Read Psalm 84 and then below write a symbolic word or phrase used in this song and what
you think those words might represent.
Note: If you have a Bible with some footnotes and commentary, it may be able to give you a
hand with some of the more obscure symbols. Check the margins and footnotes.

Symbolic Words	My Best Guess at a Meaning
Example: "My soul yearns, even faints"	I want it really, really badly

A Forgiven Heart

INTRODUCTION

Instincts are good things. It is our instinct that makes us speed up our bike peddling when a vicious dog comes barking out of nowhere. It is our instinct that moves our feet toward the brakes at the sight of a police car . . . even if we are going the speed limit.

The Christian has a certain instinct. This instinct is sparked when we consider God's mercy, forgiveness and love or things like his sacrifice on the cross for us personally. Our instinct is to worship him.

It is in worship that we come to more nearly understand God's grace and mercy. It is in the experience of worship that the weight of what was done on a dumping ground of a hill outside of Jerusalem comes into focus.

Grooming the instinct to worship God is the aim of this session: not only desiring to worship him in a corporate setting, surrounded by fellow believers, but also privately, quietly, reverently.

Christ's sacrifice on the cross is the route by which the impulses of this divine instinct very often travel. Your students will be challenged to reconsider what the gift on the cross means to them and what their proper response ought to be.

STRIKING THE MATCH

① You Want My What???

Direct your students to the student sheet on page 25 of this book. Ask them to consider who they would be willing to give one of their kidneys to if they needed it. Discuss the results and talk about which people they would and would not sacrifice for and why.

Transition from this introductory activity to what Jesus did for us by saying, **"Most of us would—perhaps with some hesitation—give away one of our kidneys to a loved one or family member. We might possibly do the same for a friend. Few of us would be willing to do it for the town drunk or some monster of a human being. When we consider that Jesus gave not just a part of himself but his whole life for those who made themselves his enemies, we can see the amazing love and sacrifice of God in action."**

LESSON FOCUS
God's forgiveness and mercy are great reasons to worship him.

LESSON GOALS
As a result of participating in this lesson, students will:
- Consider how Christ paid for our sins.
- List the ways that God shows his love and mercy towards us.
- Celebrate his sacrifice by worship.

Materials needed:
Reproducible student sheet on page 25 of this book; writing utensils

② You're on File

Give your students a short lesson in the financial facts of life as a lead into this session. Begin this activity by showing the credit report to your students. Then ask them some of these questions:

- **How many of you have a credit card in your name only?**
- **Who thinks that they will probably someday get a loan or a credit card?**
- **What are some things that would happen if you were late making your payment or defaulted on any kind of a loan or credit card?**
- **What is a credit report?**
- **If you have a bad credit history, what does that mean?**
- **How long do you think it would take to clear up a problem with your credit?**
- **How does it make you feel knowing that some agency like TRW knows everything about your financial history?**

Conclude this activity by saying, "Imagine what it would be like if God kept his own version of a credit report on people. Every time they messed up, it would be noted. It would not take most of us long to be on the divine blacklist.

"The fact is that Christ came to pay off the debt we created, debt that we could never pay off. He came to pay it off before we were even willing to change our spending habits of sin. Today we are going to consider and celebrate that action of love and mercy from God to debtors like ourselves."

FANNING THE FLAME

① How Does He Love Thee?

Ask your students to read Psalm 117 and Psalm 130 and then break into groups of four to six, perhaps grouping by favorite "love" story from Scripture: Ruth and Naomi, Jacob and Rachel, Solomon and the bride who inspired his Song of Solomon, Sarah and Abraham, etc. Give each group some poster board and felt pens. Ask each group to examine the text for several key words (hope, forgiveness, love, etc.,) and to make an acrostic for each word describing ways that God does that in our lives.

Example:

    Help for living
    Offered himself as our sacrifice
    Pays attention to our prayers
    HE gives full redemption

Ask your students to share with the group what they have created. Post the acrostics around the room.

② The Stain of Sin

Before class, prepare a number of small bottles with a palette of food coloring in them and have a marker and label handy to put the name of students entering on each bottle. On the day you plan to teach this session, make sure to wear clothes that you don't mind disposing of. You may want to have a plastic tarp ready in the event there are drips and splashes from this stunt.

Introduce your students to Psalm 130 by having a student stand and read it aloud.

Tell your students: **"We can see from this Psalm God's great love for us and his willingness to forgive us for our sins. That forgiveness came at a price because each of us has stained ourselves with impure thoughts and actions."**

At this point, pull out your small bottles of food coloring. Taking one, read off the name of the student on it and say, **"This bottle represents all the stuff you have done to discolor your life. Left on your own, your life is stained, tainted and cut off from a relationship with God. But Christ's sacrificial death has taken the stain and sin that should be upon you and has poured it out on himself."**

Next, pass out the little bottles of food coloring to each of your students and say, **"Today each of you holds a small bottle that represents your sin and failure to live the way God wants you to. I want you to get a mental picture of what incredible love God has for you. I am going to represent Christ. I want you to consider what kind of real sins might lie in the stain bottle of your life; then come up one at a time and pour out that stain on me."**

Step onto the tarp or plastic sheet and ask your students to go ahead and do their worst. This process may become humorous or it may be very serious, depending on the nature of your students. Either way, the mental picture of you drenched with various colors representing their sin will not be lost on them.

Finish your session in your discolored state. It will make the point.

DIVINE HEARTBURN

① Hand and Heart

Listen to the song "Psalm 130," by One Eighty. Check out the words on an overhead or the lyric sheet from page 77 and have your group create hand movements to go along with the lyrics.

Tell your students something like this: **"Ancient worshipers often used dance steps or hand motions to help emphasize the truth of the song they were singing. Let's see if we can invent some movements to this song of praise and worship by the ska band One Eighty."**

Give your students some time to come up with motions for the song and then play or sing the song using the hand movements. Encourage them to sketch out the movements on the student sheet on page 26 before trying the song with those moves. Close in prayer.

Materials needed:
Bibles; small bottles; food coloring; markers; stick-on labels; plastic tarp; old clothes

Try This . . .

Materials needed:
TV; VCR; the video *Amistad*

Remind your students of the wonderful love and mercy shown by Christ by using a clip from the Steven Spielberg movie, *Amistad*, found approximately 140 minutes in the movie.

The *Amistad* was a ship full of African men and woman bound for slavery in the new world. Remarkably, they managed to get control of the ship and wound up with a not-so-welcoming reception in the northeast U.S.A. During this scene, one of the Africans, illiterate but given a Bible by an abolitionist, gains an understanding of the gospel message and Christ's sacrifice by merely studying the illustrations in the text. It is a powerful piece of filmwork.

After you have shown the clip, ask students to discuss these questions:

- **How did the gospel get through to this illiterate man?**
- **What does that tell you about the nature of the "good news"?**
- **How did this man, who had suffered so much, find comfort in the gospel message?**
- **Do you think that this prisoner knew enough about Christ to put his trust in him?**

Materials needed:
CD player; CD packaged with this book; reproducible student sheet on page 26 and lyric sheet on page 77 of this book; writing utensils

Thoughts on Worship

"When God answers a prayer of my heart, I am usually so grateful and relieved that it feels like the most natural thing in the world to praise and thank him. I am especially drawn to praise and worship when I see God work in the life of someone I have been praying for, like when a friend gets saved. Just a few weeks ago, I found out that a friend I had been praying for (for over two years) had been saved out of a homosexual lifestyle. I was so excited, touched and shocked all at the same time, that I just cried and thanked God. I know I can expect God to answer my prayers, and I try to believe in faith that he will, but sometimes it still surprises me when he comes through so miraculously. When my prayers are answered, I am reminded of his goodness and love for me. It stirs the desire of my heart for him."
—Sierra Hart

② Words to Enter and Go By

Play or sing the song "Psalm 130," by One Eighty. Ask your students to read through the lyrics (which are right out of Psalm 117 and 130) and select one or two that might serve as a motto or theme for your group. For example, "With You There Is Forgiveness" or "In Your Word I Put My Hope."

Distribute poster board and colored markers. Ask your students to write the verses on the boards and then post them over the exit and entrance of the room as a reminder of what was studied today.

MIDWEEK OPTION

Forgiveness Party

Create a party at someone's home just like the one thrown for the prodigal, complete with the fatted calf (or chicken) on the BBQ.

Send out invitations to your students. Invite them to come as they are or dare them to come filthy. Pick up some cheap rings at a toy store or discount store and put one on the finger of each person who attends. If you can afford it, print up some T-shirts and hand out the "new clothes" to each person when they come.

Celebrate God's love and forgiveness with a meal and a time of worship, praise and partying.

You Want My What???

Somebody wants what you have, but you probably don't want to give it to them.

With the great advancement in organ transplants, there are now more people waiting for donor organs than there are donors to give them.

Suppose you knew that by donating a kidney (you have two but could live OK with one) you would save a person's life. Would you do it?

In the space below, write down the name of someone you would, *without hesitation,* be willing to donate a kidney to.

In the next space, write down the name of a couple of people you *might* be willing to donate a hunk of yourself to.

In the last space, write down the name of someone who in *no way* would ever get one of your kidneys.

Without Hesitation

____

Maybe, Maybe Not

____

Not a Chance

____

Psalm 130:1-8
A song of ascents.
"Out of the depths I cry to you, O LORD; O Lord, hear my voice. Let your ears be attentive to my cry for mercy.
If you, O LORD, kept a record of sins, O Lord, who could stand?
But with you there is forgiveness; therefore you are feared.
I wait for the LORD, my soul waits, and in his word I put my hope.
My soul waits for the Lord more than watchmen wait for the morning, more than watchmen wait for the morning.
O Israel, put your hope in the LORD, for with the LORD is unfailing love and with him is full redemption.
He himself will redeem Israel from all their sins."

Psalm 117:1, 2
"Praise the LORD, all you nations;
extol him, all you peoples.
For great is his love toward us,
and the faithfulness of the LORD
    endures forever.
Praise the LORD."

Hand and Heart

Work out some hand or body motions to insert along the way as you sing this song. Draw a stick figure to show what ideas you have.

"Psalm 130"

Music © 1999 Thirsty moon river publishing (ASCAP)

[VERSE 1]:

Out of the depths I cry to You, O Lord.

Lord, hear my voice,

Let Your ears be attentive to my cry

For mercy, for mercy, for mercy.

If You, O Lord, kept a record of sins,

Lord, who could stand?

But with You there is forgiveness, therefore

You are feared, You are feared, You are feared.

[CHORUS]:

Praise the Lord, all you nations extol Him,

All you peoples, for great is His love toward us.

The faithfulness of the Lord endures forever,

Praise the Lord, praise the Lord.

[VERSE 2]:

I wait for the Lord

And in His Word I put my hope.

My soul waits for the Lord

More than watchmen wait for the morning,

I wait for the Lord.

O Israel, put your hope in the Lord,

For with the Lord is unfailing love

And full redemption.

He Himself will redeem Israel

From all their sins.

A Hungry Heart

INTRODUCTION

Desiring God is the usually stated prerequisite for worship. A spiritual hunger or thirst for those things higher and greater than our mortal minds can consume draws us to throne territory. Most of us probably come to discover our hunger and desire in the midst of worship. Just as the smell of a great meal ignites the appetite we didn't realize we had, entering into worship somehow focuses our thought and lifts our hearts to another level.

One of the reasons that many of us don't sense the gnawing of spiritual hunger in our souls is the fact that we have loaded up on the world's junk food. Our minutes and hours are loaded with bits of information, distractions and tidbits that won't allow the mind to pause and consider God.

The tragedy in our fast-paced info-overload lifestyle is that most of what we mentally consume fails to satisfy us. The thoughts are void of eternal nutrients and the materials needed to equip and strengthen us.

The satisfaction that comes from hungering after God and his Word offers us the opposite. It fills and fulfills. It invigorates our lives and gives our hearts peace and contentment.

This session is designed to encourage your students to set aside the pandemonium of modern lifestyles in order to place their focus and thoughts on the One who will fill their heart and souls with himself.

STRIKING THE MATCH

① *What I Wouldn't Give for a Fish Taco*

Using a chalkboard or large sheet of paper, ask your students to help you list some food item that for them is a delicious rarity—something they don't get very often but salivate for! This may gross out some (after all, who really longs for pickled pigs feet?) and may make others hungry by just talking about it.

After they have completed the list, guide them into the next section by saying, **"Just like foods that we desire, God wants to be the longing and desire of our hearts. He wants us to have a hungry heart for him. Let's take a look at how this idea is expressed in the Psalms."**

Materials needed:
Chalkboard or butcher paper; chalk or felt-tip pen

Try This . . .

Why "All Lids"?

② Hill of Gold

Direct your students to the student sheet on page 31 of this book. Ask them to read the story, then ask them these questions:

- **How would it make you feel if you were a member of the family in the story?**
- **How would even a small portion of the wealth from the Hill of Gold have changed their lives?**
- **What are some things that we might ignore or take for granted that would give us great new opportunities or adventures if we were to dig for them?**

Conclude this activity by saying, **"Many of us have been told for years about how rich our lives can be if we spend time with God. Sometimes those words can have about as much real impact on us as the words 'Hill of Gold' did on that poor family in the story. Let's take some time this morning and see what a songwriter from many years ago had to say about where we can find true and lasting wealth for our heart . . . if we are willing to dig for it."**

FANNING THE FLAME

① Satisfied?

Direct your students to Psalm 63. Ask them to work in pairs to complete the student sheet on page 32. Your students should be able to discuss the meaning behind the imagery used in this Psalm and the feelings that the writer vents verse by verse. Ask them to:

- **Describe some of the images found in this Psalm. What do they stand for?**
- **Describe some of the feelings that the author let come out as he penned this song.**

Play the song "All Lids," by Soul-Junk (see the side margin for the reason the band called this musical version of Psalm 63 by that name).

After you have played the song, ask your group:

- **Do you think that a hunger for God is a natural occurrence for most people? Why or why not?**
- **What might spoil a person's appetite for God?**
- **What does this Psalm tell you about things that satisfy and things that don't?**

② What Can Satisfy?

On a chalkboard, write this famous quote by Augustine: "If God Himself can't satisfy us, what else possibly could?" Direct your students' attention to this by asking:

- **Do you agree or disagree with this observation?**
- **What kind of meaning or implications do you draw from this statement?**

Divide your class into groups of four to six students, possibly by encouraging them to select their favorite thirst-quencher: water, soda or fruit juice. Ask the groups to read Psalm 63 and assign each group one of the following:

• Create a skit or drama that demonstrates how some people may "spoil their appetite" for God by filling their lives with other less satisfying things.

• Using stacks of old magazines, scissors and glue, create a collage of cutout pictures illustrating things with which people fill their lives that don't really satisfy a person's heart and soul.

• Read through the Psalm and find a passage that could serve as a motto for your group. Have everyone write the motto on a piece of cardstock and take it home with them to post in their rooms.

After fifteen or twenty minutes, have your students share what they have been assigned with the rest of the group.

DIVINE HEARTBURN

① *Makin' a Pledge*

Distribute to each student a 3" x 5" card and a marker and ask everyone to write down a pledge or promise to God that they will do to attempt to "fill themselves with him." It should be something that they will strive to do in order to help themselves stay hungry for him. Encourage them to make it practical. (Example: Turn off the CD player for awhile when I am driving and just talk to God.) Remind them to be sure to date and sign their promise.

Close by leading a prayer. Then, if you have not already used it in your session, play or sing as a closing song "All Lids (Psalm 63)," by the band Soul-Junk. Make sure you have copies of the words on a lyric sheet or on an overhead transparency. Ask students to make the song their prayer as they sing or listen to it being performed.

② *Personal Praise*

Ask your students to listen to how the psalmist expresses his ideas of worship for God. Play the song "All Lids (Psalm 63)," by the band Soul-Junk. Make sure you have copies of the words on a lyric sheet or on an overhead transparency.

After you have listened to this rendition of Psalm 63, distribute paper and writing utensils to each student. Ask your group to join you in an act of worship that can be both personal and powerful. Tell students, **"I am going to read the beginning of several sentences about God. Please finish each sentence with a word or two that come into your heart and mind as an act of adoration of God."**

Try reading some of the following:

• **God, you are _______________________.**
• **I thank you for your __________________ to me.**
• **I desire to ___________________.**
• **When I consider You, I __________________.**
• **___________________ reminds me of your greatness.**
• **___________________ reminds me of your love.**

Materials needed:
Markers; 3" x 5" cards; overhead or reproducible lyric sheet on page 78 of this book; CD player; CD packaged with this book

Thoughts on Worship

"One of the church's most intense needs today is to feed the 'come let us return to the Lord' dynamic (Hosea 6:1) as deep as we possibly can. If God spent so much time instructing Moses and David concerning how to use music in temple worship, then we need to understand that he's got ideas and instruction for us now that we have no concept of. Anyone who loves God and loves music today should be asking God for that instruction and the inspiration to bring it to life."—Glen Galloway of Soul-Junk

Materials needed:
Reproducible lyric sheet on page 78 of this book; CD player; CD packaged with this book; paper; writing utensils

You can add more ideas to the ones above by merely combing through the Psalms. You may wish to ask students to share what they have written or merely allow these word offerings to remain private and close in prayer.

Hill of Gold

A True Story

In 1978 a poor Afghani family crawled from the squalor of their primitive one-room hut to stare at the plumes of dust coming their way across the barren desert.

They had lived for years at the foot of this mound in the desert called "Tillya Tepe" and now the small little hill had visitors: archeologists. With shovels, picks and finally brushes and sifters, they managed to unearth an incredible array of golden treasure.

The family watched awestruck as each magnificent and priceless find was dislodged from centuries of hiding underground . . . just a stroll from their ramshackle home.

Merely one of those artifacts would have burst the bonds of poverty and despair that had trapped the family for decades. What made it worse was the fact that even though the family knew that the name of the mound "Tillya Tepe" meant Hill of Gold, they had never bothered to take it seriously.

How would it make you feel if you were part of this family?

Knowing what the name of the hill was, do you think you would have done any poking around if you had lived there?

Can you think of opportunities that people in your world might have missed by ignoring them or taking them for granted?

"I am in awe of God . . . in so many ways."
—Justin Bundschuh of Spooky Tuesday

Satisfied:

A look at King David's journal while he was hiding out

Psalm 63:1-11

A psalm of David. When he was in the desert of Judah.

"O God, you are my God, earnestly I seek you; my soul thirsts for you, my body longs for you, in a
  dry and weary land where there is no water.
I have seen you in the sanctuary and beheld your power and your glory.
Because your love is better than life, my lips will glorify you.
I will praise you as long as I live, and in your name I will lift up my hands.
My soul will be satisfied as with the richest of foods; with singing lips my mouth will praise you.
On my bed I remember you; I think of you through the watches of the night.
Because you are my help, I sing in the shadow of your wings.
I stay close to you; your right hand upholds me.
They who seek my life will be destroyed; they will go down to the depths of the earth.
They will be given over to the sword and become food for jackals.
But the king will rejoice in God; all who swear by God's name will praise him, while the mouths of liars will be
  silenced."

Read Psalm 63 and then take a crack at filling in the blanks of David's journal with the words
from this Psalm that you think fit the best.

MAY 14TH

IT'S BEEN A TOUGH DAY. HERE I AM IN THE MIDDLE OF THE DESERT, SCARED AND DISCOURAGED,
BUT YET . . .

JUST TODAY, THE HOT WINDS AND MEAGER FOOD MADE ME THINK THAT . . .

EVEN THOUGH MY STOMACH IS HUNGRY, I KNOW THAT . . .

I TELL MY MEN . . .

IT MAKES THEM SMILE TO THINK . . .

REAL LATE AT NIGHT . . .

> "Every experience we have is meant to teach us more about worship—even things like getting torn up emotionally or being strongly tempted. God wants this stuff to drive us into the incredible life we have with him in the Spirit."
> —Glen Galloway of Soul-Junk

A Soothed Heart

INTRODUCTION

We use some interesting phrases when it comes to talking about our hearts. We say "I have a heavy heart," "What a real sweetheart she is" or "He's just heartsick about it" as if the organ whose purpose is to circulate the liquid of life actually has the dynamic of emotions.

Of course what we mean by these kinds of descriptions is that our emotional state is either joyful, contented, upset, frozen, despairing or in some other kind of bliss or turmoil. *Heart* is a shortcut term that we all understand.

When our hearts are wrenched and racked with pain, guilt or trouble, we seek relief. Psychologists and self-help authors have made their fortunes attempting to salve the pain of a heart in misery. But it's the authors of the Psalms who present to us the ultimate refuge for our emotional turbulence—God himself.

STRIKING THE MATCH

1. How Do You Spell Relief?

Distribute copies of the student sheet on page 37 and ask your students to work individually to describe how they find relief in the areas stated. (Be prepared for some off-the-wall discussion.)

Allow your students to share a few of the things they have written with the rest of your group. Move on to the next section of this lesson by saying something like this: **"We humans dislike being uncomfortable. While there are plenty of things to make us feel the need for relief, there is nothing that can make a person more uncomfortable than being burdened with guilt and sin. Today we are going to look at a Psalm that celebrates God's relief-giving and burden-lifting pardon and the joy that comes from walking close to him daily."**

LESSON FOCUS

Our hearts are encouraged when we are in a close relationship with God.

LESSON GOALS

As a result of participating in this lesson, students will:

- Describe what God does to give our hearts relief and encouragement.
- Discuss the reasons a person's heart gets heavy.
- Have an opportunity to memorize a portion of Psalm 32 for heart strength.

Materials needed:
Reproducible student sheet on page 37 of this book; writing utensils

Try This . . .

2 How Much Can You Carry?

Before your meeting, collect a box full of objects that students can pass to one another. When you are ready to start your meeting, have all of the students stand in a circle. Begin by giving a student one object with the instructions to merely pass it around the circle. If anyone drops the object, he is out of the game. Once the game starts, as quickly as you can begin to add items to pass. If you have enough items of various shapes and sizes, it will be just a matter of time before someone fumbles them. Pull the student out of the circle and keep going. The smaller the circle, the quicker people will fumble.

Play the game until you have either reduced the circle to a couple of people or until you have a solid core of jugglers left. Congratulate the winners and give them some sort of prize.

Conclude this activity by saying, **"Many people find that the things life hands to them become too much to handle. They fumble and mess up. Today we are going to examine a Psalm that gives us encouragement for the times we foul up and find ourselves too weak to handle what we have been given."**

FANNING THE FLAME

1 Truth That Sticks

Ahead of time, you will need to purchase some adhesive-backed paper, which can be found at a large office supply store. Cut blank bumper stickers from this paper, enough for every student to have one.

Begin this activity by asking your students to read Psalm 32 and to create slogans for bumper stickers that come from the various ideas in that Psalm. The slogans should sum up a moral or another concept found in the Scripture passage. Distribute the supplies and have students create their stickers.

After they have completed their work, let them share their creations.

Ask questions such as these:

- **What impression of personal experience does the writer seem to describe?**
- **What does the writer want to encourage people to do?**

Play the Havalina Rail Co. version of the classic song "Just a Closer Walk With Thee" or have your own worship team perform it. Ask your students to pay close attention to the words (hand them out or put them on the overhead).

After the song, try out these questions for discussion:

- **How does a person have a close walk with God?**
- **What are some tips that you might give a person who seemed to find it difficult to have a consistent devotional time?**
- **What hinders a person from being close with God?**

② Picture That!

Ask your students to break into groups of three to five, perhaps by having them respond to photos of restful places: a deserted beach, mountaintop, church sanctuary, quiet stream, etc. Have each group read Psalm 32 and then create a symbol for various ideas stated in that Psalm. (For example, someone might write "1-2-3" with a universal "no" symbol for the idea that God does not *count* our sin against us in verse two. Another student might draw a bone for the expression of "wasting bones" in verse three.)

Ask your students to hold up the symbols they have created and tell what concept each represents in the Psalm.

Note: You can take this idea to another level by grabbing some coat hangers and string and creating a Psalm 32 mobile.

Materials needed:
Bibles; a stack of cardstock; scissors; felt-tip pens

DIVINE HEARTBURN

① A Word Hidden in the Heart

The Psalms are full of great passages to commit to memory. Ask your students to comb through Psalm 32 and find a couple of verses that stand out to them as points of encouragement. Then give them enough time to memorize the verses they have chosen.

You may also want to provide tools to make the memorization process easier. Small stickers or business-card size pieces of paper with the verse on it can be posted where they will be readily viewed, or you may choose to use the "Memory Checker" student sheet on page 38.

Materials needed:
Inkjet business-card blanks, blank stickers or Post-it™ notes; writing utensils; or reproducible student sheet on page 38 of this book

② A Song From the Heart

Ask your group to sing along as you play the song "Just a Closer Walk With Thee" on the HeartBurn CD. Use these questions to help students reflect on the ideas presented in the song:

- **What would make your walk closer with Jesus?**
- **If you thought of "walking with Jesus" as a journey, what might you pack that would make the walk more difficult?**
- **What is the attitude the songwriter displays about himself? Why is there strength in realizing our weaknesses?**

If your group is too small or musically impaired, simply read the words as a closing prayer, then conclude by playing the CD again.

Thoughts on Worship

"For whatever reason, God has made us as people to reflect him. He is creative and made us like him in this way; he has endowed human beings with creativity. It is our duty and spiritual nature to give back to him some part of what he has created in us—that's why music is such a vital part of worship. As it says in one of the old confessions, 'The sole purpose of man is to love God and enjoy him forever.' Worshiping him in musical creation is a part of the love and enjoying."—Matt Wignall of Havalina Rail Co.

Materials needed:
CD player; CD packaged with this book; reproducible lyric sheet on page 78 of this book

Next to the Skin

If you want to try something really fun, use Psalm 32 or the words from "Just a Closer Walk With Thee" (or any of the other passages or songs in this course) as the basis for a temporary tattoo.

Work with any student or adult who has a design program on his computer (Corel Draw, Adobe Illustrator, Photoshop or the like) and a color printer to come up with a design that you could convert to a tattoo. Have them printed and pass them out to your youth group.

You can order 1000 full-color tattoos (enough for the whole church and then some) for under $200. Try these two companies for starters: Calico Temporary Tattoos, 3000 Alamo Drive, Suite 201, Vacaville, California 95687, (707) 448-7072 or fax (707) 446-8273; or The Sticker Guys at info@stickerguys.com or (888) 644-7745.

How Do You Spell
Relief?

Write down what you do to get relief when or if . . .

• You hit the wall doing your homework and can't think anymore

• Your arm or leg falls asleep

• You are getting seasick or carsick

• You have an itch where you can't reach it

• You can't find any clean underwear

• You can't use the phone because your sister is hogging it

• You are dog tired but don't want to fall asleep in church or class

• You are on a long car trip with people who love music you despise

• You have a gnarly sunburn

• You find yourself lost in a strange city

• You find everyone staring at you for the dumb comment you just made

• You are bored, bored, bored

> *"Having the pride or arrogance to be bitter at God for situations that happen in our lives plays havoc with our ability to worship God."*
> *—Matt Wignall of Havalina Rail Co.*

Psalm 32:1-11
Of David. A *maskil*.

"Blessed is he whose transgressions are forgiven, whose sins are covered.
Blessed is the man whose sin the LORD does not count against him and in whose spirit is no deceit.
When I kept silent, my bones wasted away through my groaning all day long.
For day and night your hand was heavy upon me; my strength was sapped as in the heat of summer.
Selah
Then I acknowledged my sin to you and did not cover up my iniquity. I said, 'I will confess my transgressions
    to the LORD'—and you forgave the guilt of my sin.
Selah
Therefore let everyone who is godly pray to you while you may be found; surely when the mighty waters rise,
    they will not reach him.
You are my hiding place; you will protect me from trouble and surround me with songs of deliverance.
Selah
I will instruct you and teach you in the way you should go; I will counsel you and watch over you.
Do not be like the horse or the mule, which have no understanding but must be controlled by bit and bridle or
    they will not come to you.
Many are the woes of the wicked, but the LORD's unfailing love surrounds the man who trusts in him.
Rejoice in the LORD and be glad, you righteous; sing, all you who are upright in heart!"

Write the verse or verses that you plan to memorize in the space below. Then each day see if you can say that bit of Scripture without looking it up first. If you pulled it off, check the box.

Verses
❏ Sunday

❏ Monday

❏ Tuesday

❏ Wednesday

❏ Thursday

❏ Friday

❏ Saturday

Use the tear sheets below to help you memorize passages from the Psalms that you would like to keep stored in your head. Write each of the verses on a slip of paper, cut them out, and then post them where you are likely to see them: mirrors, light switch, bedpost, etc.

A Thankful Heart

INTRODUCTION

It is easy to become jaded. We live our lives wishing for a little more rather than standing in awe at the incredible fortune that God has poured out on us. This is especially true of those who are raised in North America, Australia, New Zealand and Western Europe. The cornucopia of opportunities we enjoy is mind-boggling in contrast with the dreary and dangerous manner of life lived by the rest of the world. To contemplate it can either drench us with guilt or spur us to generous actions and gratitude to God.

But because the rest of the world is out of sight and only invades our lives as some kind of easy-to-switch-off-feed-the-children TV plea, many in our culture and even in our churches lean towards gluttonous and ungrateful hearts.

The early Psalm writers lived out their lives closer to the ragged edge. They understood what could happen if there was a season without rain or if an invading tribe appeared on the horizon. Because of this tenuous lifestyle, thanksgiving for the things we pampered moderns take for granted was quickly on their lips.

The intent of this session is to bring your students' view of the world and their gifts and responsibilities back into focus, with the hope that this clear picture might prompt them to worship God with true thanksgiving and act out that gratefulness in ways that make a difference.

LESSON FOCUS
A thankful heart is an essential part of true worship.

LESSON GOALS
As a result of participating in this lesson, students will:
- Consider how bountifully they are blessed in contrast with most of the world's people.
- List some things for which they are personally grateful.
- Take an action that demonstrates their thankfulness to others.

STRIKING THE MATCH

① Lucky Moves

Ahead of time, pick up an inexpensive game of checkers and doctor each game piece with words or statements that represent things in life that we have but often take for granted. Use small round stickers or just tape small squares of paper to each piece. Use words such as home, health, food, friends, long life, money, education, freedom and so forth. Stick the same list on both the black and red checkers.

Set up the checkerboard on a table. On the chalkboard, write all of the blessings you have listed on the game pieces. Now you are ready to play.

When your group assembles, tell the students: **"Today we are going to play a game of checkers, girls against guys, to see which group**

Materials needed:
Game of checkers; small stickers; felt-tip pen; table; chalk and chalkboard

Materials needed:
Reproducible student sheet on page 43 of this book

Materials needed:
Bibles; CD player; CD packaged with this book; reproducible lyric sheet on page 79 of this book; writing utensils

can end the game with most of their 'lives' intact. You see, on each checker is a word showing some item that we often take for granted in life. Your objective is to try to keep as many of these attributes as you can while eliminating them in your opponent.

"Here are the rules. Girls use the red pieces. The girls go first. If there is a jump, you MUST take it. For each move, a different person will come to the table and have 30 seconds to study the board and make a move. I will count down the last five seconds. If the player does not move by the end of 30 seconds, I will remove the game piece from the board that is the furthest from home. At the end of the game, the loser will be dead or trapped and I will cross off on the chalkboard all the attributes the winning team has lost by moves of the other team."

Play the game with your group. At the end of the game, note that one person has vanished and the other has made it through but at the cost of many things we take for granted. Cross the lost pieces off your posted list.

Continue with the next section by saying, **"While this is just a dumb game for us, for many in the world life has not been as kind. Millions of people barely make it through life with all of the things you and I take for granted. Today we are going to consider just how much God has blessed us with and the natural burst of worship for him that should follow."**

② *Swallow These Stats*

Ask your students to take a look at statistics on page 43 of this book. Discuss the impact of these troubling statistics with these questions:
- **Who was aware of this information?**
- **Would you agree or disagree with the idea that those of us who have been given much are required to do much?**
- **What are the feelings you get when you realize the difference between your life and that of a person in the Third World?**

Conclude this activity by saying, **"One of the things that typifies the attitude of a person who is seeking after God is a sense of thankfulness and gratitude for all the things God has done for him or her. Having considered just how incredibly blessed we are, let's take a look at a Psalm that comes from that same spirit."**

FANNING THE FLAME

① *A New Song*

Read Psalm 100 with your students. Then teach and sing (or play for) your students the song titled, "A Brighter Way," by Sierra Hart. It is recorded on the CD that was packaged with this book.

Ask your students to work in small groups to add lyrics to Sierra's song that express ideas of thankfulness coming from their lives. Ask everyone to share their new lyrics. If you have the musicians do it, sing the song again using the new lyrics as well as the original ones.

② *Thankful in Every Direction*

Read Psalm 100 and follow it by singing "A Brighter Way," by Sierra Hart. Discuss some of the things that both songwriters, the Psalmist and Sierra, give thanks for. Then ask your students to work on the "Thankful Crossword" student sheet on page 44. Tape each sheet around the room as your students finish so that others can see what their friends are thankful to God for.

Materials needed:
Bibles; reproducible student sheet on page 44 of this book; reproducible lyric sheet on page 79; writing utensils; masking tape

DIVINE HEARTBURN

① *Action Thanks*

Begin this activity by saying, **"What better way to show our gratitude to God than by a thank offering of action—doing something for someone else motivated strictly by the desire to demonstrate our thanksgiving to God. Help me brainstorm a list of practical things we could do as a group (or as individuals) that would help someone or the church and yet be an offering of our appreciation to God."**

Materials needed:
Chalk; chalkboard

As your students brainstorm, record their list on the chalkboard. After each idea is shared, ask what practical steps it would take to put that idea into action. For example, if students decide to wash the windows of someone's home or some part of the church, set the time, place and designate a materials list before ending the session.

One great project might be to sponsor, as a group, a child in a Third World country. A very reliable organization which does a great job providing those services and ways for sponsors to stay in touch with their child through mail and e-mail is *Compassion International*. Contact them and see about sponsoring a child. For less than a buck a day, your group can help change a life! Contact them at (800) 336-7676 or check out their web site at http://www.ci.org.

Close in prayer.

② *A Plate Full of Thanks*

Hand out slips of paper and pens or pencils to your students. Ask them to write down a word of thanksgiving on the slip of paper. For example, someone might write: "I thank God for having an opportunity to know and enjoy my grandparents."

Encourage your students to take the slips of paper to a worship service with them and to prayerfully slip them into the offering plate along with whatever monies they may give as an offering of thanks to God. Clue in the minister and money counters about what may be coming along with the checks.

Close in prayer.

Thoughts on Worship

"I am a 'to-do list' kind of girl, and so often, I feel like I have to cross 10 things off my list before I can really relax, quiet down and spend some time worshiping God. Many times I'll sit down to pray with the best of intentions, and about five minutes into it, I'll think, *I should start some laundry,* or, *Oh yeah, I gotta get that letter in the mail.* I have a hard enough time sitting still to watch a movie, so it is a real challenge for me to chill out and give God the time he wants and deserves. Honestly, when I go to spend time with God, I usually have to force myself, because it seems like there are so many other things I would rather do first. But after a few minutes, I settle down, and I remember how good it is to be with God, and how unimportant everything else is in light of his presence."
—Sierra Hart

Materials needed:
Slips of paper; writing utensils

Swallow ·············· *These* ·········· Stats

Here are the facts about how a huge bulk of the children in the world live. You might be vaguely aware of a gap in lifestyles . . . but now you have the real numbers.

- More than 130 million six to eleven year olds do not attend school in the developing countries.
- Nearly two-thirds of these children are girls.
- In just the past ten years, the estimated impact of armed conflict on children includes two million killed, six million seriously injured or permanently disabled, 12 million left homeless, more than one million orphaned or separated from their families and ten million psychologically traumatized.
- Nearly one billion people—or one-sixth of humanity—are functionally illiterate. Nearly a quarter of the world's population cannot read and write; of this population, two-thirds are women. This hard fact limits the ability of their children to escape the cycle of poverty.
- Malnutrition is implicated in more than half of all child deaths worldwide—a figure unmatched by any infectious disease since the Black Death. Of the nearly 12 million children under five who die each year in developing countries mainly from preventable diseases, the deaths of over six million, or 55 percent, are directly or indirectly caused by malnutrition.
- About 183 million children weigh less than they should for their age. One study indicated that children who were severely underweight were found to be two to eight times more likely to die within the following year as children of normal weight for their age.
- A young child dies of malaria every 30 seconds.
- The International Labour Organization estimates that there are 250 million children working full- or part-time in the developing world. Work prevents many children from receiving an education or gaining from it.
- An estimated 300,000 children around the world are fighting the wars of adults.

Sources: UNICEF's *The State of the World's Children* 1999 & 1998 reports; World Health Organization

Now, ask yourself these questions:

- **Was I aware of most of this information?**

- **Would I agree or disagree with the idea that those of us who have been given much are required to do much?**

- **What are the feelings I get when I realize the difference between my life and that of a person in the Third World?**

Wanna do something about it? Contact Compassion International and see about sponsoring a child. For less than a buck a day, you can help change a life! Call them at (800) 336-7676 or check out their website at http://www.ci.org.

A Thankful Crossword

Psalm 100:1-5

A psalm. For giving thanks.

"Shout for joy to the LORD, all the earth.
Serve the LORD with gladness; come before him with joyful songs.
Know that the LORD is God. It is he who made us, and we are his; we are his
    people, the sheep of his pasture.
Enter his gates with thanksgiving and his courts with praise; give thanks to him
    and praise his name.
For the LORD is good and his love endures forever; his faithfulness continues
    through all generations."

Use the blank squares below to create as many words as possible in a
crossword form that represent things you are thankful to God for. See if
you can fill up the page. Be ready to let others know what you are grateful
for.

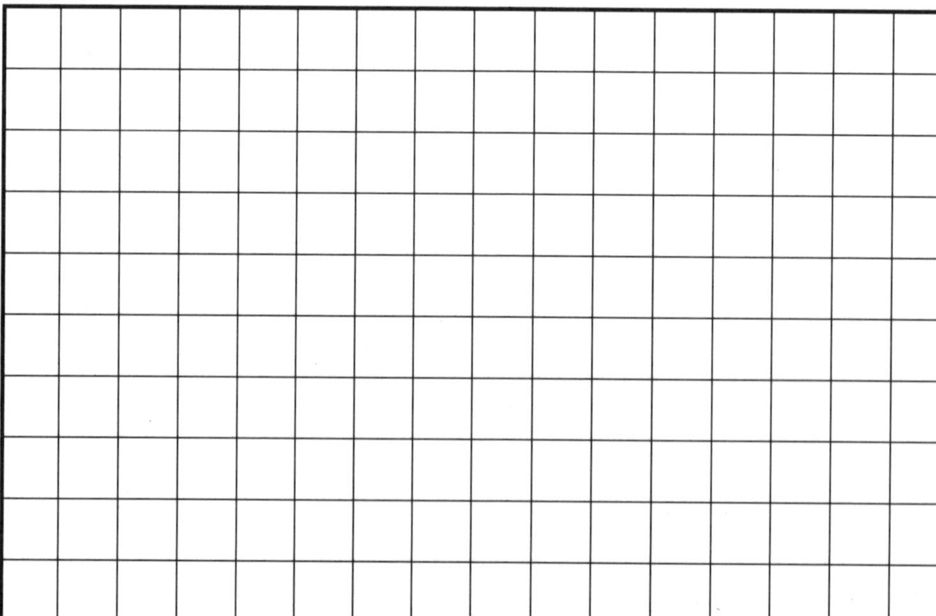

An Offered Heart

INTRODUCTION

"What good will it be for a man if he gains the whole world, yet forfeits his soul? Or what can a man give in exchange for his soul?" (Matthew 16:26).

Leave it up to Jesus to pose a really good question, a question that has provoked writers and filmmakers to come up with a variety of stories based on an evil exchange: a human soul to the devil for some instant gift or gratification.

The human soul belongs to God. It is given to us to use, develop and grow. We cannot keep it or extend it beyond his will.

But there is one thing we can do with our soul. We can offer the governing of it back to the one who made us. As Paul commented in Romans 12:1, ". . . this is your spiritual act of worship."

The exchange makes sense. It makes sense in terms of gratitude, a fair exchange for all we have been given. It makes sense in terms of wisdom. Trying to steer our own lives only gets us off track. It is infinitely more sensible to give up the control to God. He alone can direct us with a minimum of damage and a maximum of joy.

In this session your students will be encouraged to go all the way in worship; not just to lift their voices—but to offer their lives. They will be encouraged to make worship not something that they do but a way that they live.

STRIKING THE MATCH

1. *The Car of Your Dreams*

Make sure that all your students have pens or pencils and a copy of the student sheet on page 49. Direct them to "The Car of Your Dreams" sheet. Say, **"Imagine that an old man from your church came up to you and told you that he wanted to buy you the car of your dreams. Use this sheet to describe what you would end up with and how your relationship with this old guy might change. Be prepared to share what you've written."**

After your students have worked for a few minutes, pull the group back together and ask various students to share what they have written. Continue with the next part of the session by saying, **"You can all see that getting such a radical and unexpected gift would change our**

LESSON TEXT
Psalm 116; Romans 12:1, 2

LESSON FOCUS
Considering what God has done for us prompts us to want to honor and worship him.

LESSON GOALS
As a result of participating in this lesson, students will:
- Evaluate the riches and blessings God has provided for them.
- Describe how God has helped them in a time of trouble.
- Experience an opportunity to offer all they are to God.
- Decide specific actions to take this week in a response of gratitude to God's love.

Materials needed:
Reproducible student sheet on page 49 of this book; writing utensils

Try This . . .

Grab the classic true story of John Merrick: *The Elephant Man*. Spin the video to the section where the Elephant Man recites the Twenty-Third Psalm (which the doctor thinks he has taught him in order to make him appear to be lucid enough to merit a hospital stay). This scene is approximately fifty minutes into the film.

After showing the clip, ask students:

- **Why would this Psalm be especially meaningful for a person with a difficult life (such as John Merrick)?**

Read the Twenty-Third Psalm again and ask:

- **What lines stand out or speak most to you?**
- **What advantage is there to committing a special Psalm or part of a Psalm to memory?**

relationship with the one who gave it. Appreciation, respect, honor and gratefulness would be the natural response of a normal person. Today we are going to consider the fact that God has done far more for us than we can even imagine and we will be thinking about what our response and relationship should be towards him."

② _Who Do Ya Owe?_

Pass out 3"x 5" cards and pens or pencils to your students with these instructions: **"On these cards please write the first name of a friend or family member you feel some sense of indebtedness towards, not because you owe them money but because of something that they have done for you. For example, it could be a person who spent time teaching you some skill or encouraging you in some sport. On the back of the card, write one word to describe the area in which they are significant to you. Example: 'Joe—baseball' for Uncle Joe who taught you how to throw a spitball. Be prepared to share what you've written with the group."**

After several minutes, ask a number of students to share what they have written with the rest of the group or, if your group is large or pressed for time, ask your students to find several other students and tell them whose name they wrote and why.

Conclude this activity by saying, **"You've seen how people who contribute to our lives become significant. Today we are going to consider what God has done for us and what our response ought to be to him for his love, blessing and involvement in our lives."**

FANNING THE FLAME

① _First Person_

Before this session, line up a small number of people (adults or teens) to give a spoken or written testimony on the topic "Why I Love God" or "How God Has Been Good to Me." Ask them to read Psalm 116 before they prepare what they are going to say.

Begin this activity by reading Psalm 116 to your students. (You may want to read this Psalm in a paraphrase such as THE MESSAGE or Living Bible.) Tell your students, **"The words of this Psalm are not merely reflections of someone ages ago; they are as powerful and fresh today. I have asked a few people to comment on how God has done similar things in their lives as he did for the writer of this Psalm."**

Introduce your speakers or read what they have written to your group. Allow students to ask questions of those who are present.

After your guests have shared, ask your students to review Psalm 116 once more by asking:

- **What could be considered "chains" in a person's life?**
- **Describe the problems the psalmist had.**
- **What did God do?**
- **How did the writer say he would repay God for the love and**

mercy he was shown?

Ask your group to describe God's goodness to them in one of the following ways:

• **NEIGHBOR NUDGE**

Tell a friend on each side of you at least three ways that God has been good to you.

• **WRITTEN DECLARATION**

Pass out paper and pencils and have your students write a "Declaration of God's Love." Start it out with the words "This declaration is to state that God has been incredibly good to ______ by ______."

• **PICTURE THIS**

Toss out a pile of old magazines and scissors. Have some rubber cement handy and a large poster board. Ask students to cut out images that represent God's love and goodness to them and stick them to the board. Tape the poster board on the wall and invite students to share the significance of what has been glued there.

Move your students into personal ownership of the idea of worshiping God because of his goodness to us by saying something like this: **"As we consider all that God has done for us, it seems important that we also respond to God in some significant way. Let's consider how that might be done."**

② *Behind the Lines*

Direct your students to the "Behind the Lines" student sheet on page 50. Ask each student to work individually to come up with a fictional story that could have been behind the words of Psalm 116. Make sure that your students read their ideas to the group or share them with each other.

Then discuss these questions:
• **What could be considered "chains" in a person's life?**
• **Describe the problems the psalmist had.**
• **What did God do?**
• **How did the writer say he would repay God for the love and mercy he was shown?**

Conclude this activity by saying, **"As we consider all that God has done for us, it seems important that we also respond to God in some significant way. Let's consider how that might be done."**

DIVINE HEARTBURN

① *My Self, the Offering*

Read Romans 12:1, 2 to your group and then ask:
• **What does offering yourself as a living sacrifice to God mean to you?**

Take your students on a special adventure through the Old Testament by examining how the Hebrews expressed their worship to God in the form of sacrifices and offerings. Examine and discuss various kinds of offerings given by the people of Israel and their significance:
• Burnt offering—Leviticus 1:3, 4
• Grain offering—Leviticus 2:1
• Fellowship offering—Leviticus 3:1
• Sin offering—Leviticus 4:3
• Guilt offering—Leviticus 5:14-19
• Wave offering—Leviticus 7:31-36
• What it meant to give of the "first fruits" and how that might be an example for Christians today. See Numbers 18:12.
• Ways that Old Testament offerings might have been symbolic of the final sacrifice Christ made. See Mark 14:24; Luke 22:20; John 1:29; Hebrews 7:11-17; and 1 John 1:7.

To really go off the wall as you study this subject, dress up like a priest, set up a barbecue and send your students off to find various types of offerings illustrated in the Old Testament and cook 'em up. (Avoid sacrificing the neighborhood cat. Send students to the church refrigerator to look for hot dogs as a meat sacrifice.)

Materials needed:
Bibles; reproducible student sheet on page 50 of this book; writing utensils

Materials needed:
Bibles; CD player; CD packaged with this book; reproducible lyric sheet on page 79 of this book

Materials needed:
3" x 5" cards; writing utensils; Bibles; CD player; CD packaged with this book; reproducible lyric sheet on page 79 of this book; offering box

• **How can it be done in practical day-by-day living?**

Play the song "Offered Myself," by Spooky Tuesday. You may wish to print the words on an overhead transparency or pass them out to your students.

After your students have worshiped through the song, ask:

• **In what way could you offer yourself to God?**
• **Who would be blessed by your life if it were completely in God's hands?**
• **How would they be blessed?**
• **Why do you think it would be a wise thing for a person to offer himself daily to God?**

Conclude by asking students to make the message of this song their prayer.

② Throw in the Cards

Pass out four 3" x 5" cards to each student. Direct your group in this activity with these instructions: **"Write the name of three or four of the most significant people in your life on the first card, people you really care about, and wouldn't want to lose. On the second card, write down future goals and dreams, things you hope that you will be able to do, have or accomplish by the end of your life (for example: getting married, having a child, etc.) On the third card, write down a couple of things about yourself that you consider to be your best assets. Be honest, no false humility; no one will be seeing what you have written. On card four, write down a few material things that mean something to you—possessions, things that you would grab first if your house caught on fire."**

Ask your group to hang on to their cards. Read Romans 12:1, 2 and then play or sing the song "Offered Myself," by Spooky Tuesday. Ask your students to think quietly about what it might really mean to offer themselves to God in return for his love and grace.

Invite your students to prayerfully consider if they would be willing to offer all the things of importance in their lives, signified by the cards they are holding in their hands, to God.

Set out a box or offering basket. Have your students bow in prayer and count the cost and consider what it might really mean to give God control of all these areas. Play "Offered Myself" again and while other heads are bowed invite any who would be willing, to walk up and deposit the cards in the box as a symbol of their desire to commit all the areas of their lives to God.

Close in prayer.

Imagine that some old guy in your church came up to you and told you that he wanted to buy you "the car of your dreams." In the space below write down, describe or draw what that car might be like and what extra features you would want on it.

BEHIND THE LINES

Read Psalm 116 and then come up with a fictional story that could represent what the writer was going through. It can be a modern story but should reflect the problems and solutions described by the Psalm writer.

Psalm 116:1-19

"I love the LORD, for he heard my voice; he heard my cry for mercy.
Because he turned his ear to me, I will call on him as long as I live.
The cords of death entangled me, the anguish of the grave came upon me; I was overcome by trouble and sorrow.
Then I called on the name of the LORD: 'O LORD, save me!'
The LORD is gracious and righteous; our God is full of compassion.
The LORD protects the simplehearted; when I was in great need, he saved me.
Be at rest once more, O my soul, for the LORD has been good to you.
For you, O LORD, have delivered my soul from death, my eyes from tears, my feet from stumbling, that I may walk
    before the LORD in the land of the living.
I believed; therefore I said, 'I am greatly afflicted.'
And in my dismay I said, 'All men are liars.'
How can I repay the LORD for all his goodness to me?
I will lift up the cup of salvation and call on the name of the LORD.
I will fulfill my vows to the LORD in the presence of all his people.
Precious in the sight of the LORD is the death of his saints.
O LORD, truly I am your servant; I am your servant, the son of your maidservant; you have freed me from my chains.
I will sacrifice a thank offering to you and call on the name of the LORD.
I will fulfill my vows to the LORD in the presence of all his people, in the courts of the house of the LORD—in your
    midst, O Jerusalem.
Praise the LORD."

"*Worship is a choice—you have to decide to praise God because he deserves and loves it.*"
—Kevin Penner of Spooky Tuesday

A Worship Fest

INTRODUCTION

Students getting together for nothing other than praise and worship is becoming a wonderful occurrence all across the world. Typically, in an event like this there is no "message" other than that coming from the words to the songs. Usually there is no offering taken and not much to break the spirit of celebration created. (Some groups do work in short skits, videos clips or dramas.) You can get your students into an event like this in a number of different ways. Here are some ideas:

1 *Create Your Own*

Put together a hot praise and worship band of your own students, adults or a conglomeration of players from several churches. Use some of the songs from this course to get you started as well as others your group already knows. Even a small cluster of motivated musicians can make this event happen. Gather a group of them together and share your vision. See if it catches!

Bathe the planning and execution of the worship experience in prayer. Commit the whole thing to God. After all, it's *his* event and *his* group. You are simply a steward of that which he has entrusted to you.

Try to hold the event in a neutral and central location. A school drama room, for example, works really well for a first event as it is not as huge as an auditorium but has a stage and lights.

Make sure to have your songs on an overhead or a PowerPoint system. Have someone be in charge of making sure the sound is tight and clean.

Contact other church youth groups and invite them to attend. (Putting this kind of event on a Sunday evening or Wednesday night, a time when many youth groups typically hold meetings, actually may help your attendance as many groups are looking for something like this to join.)

If you are inviting the Christian community, try to keep what happens in your praise and worship fest appropriate for believers of different backgrounds. It is probably true that you "can't please 'em all," but excesses or denominational peculiarities should be avoided if possible.

FOCUS
Students will come together for an extended time of celebration and worship.

GOALS
As a result of this event:
- Students will have an opportunity to worship outside of the normal church context.
- Many different people in the church will be involved in this worship experience.
- Non-Christian students will be presented with the opportunity to draw near God.

Materials needed:
Photocopy the flyer on page 53 to advertise your event!

② Create With Others

Contact some other youth workers from other churches and see about making this a joint effort on the part of a number of churches. Networking is absolutely critical to youth ministry in this generation.

③ Let Someone Else Create It

Find a praise and worship fest already in progress and support it. Ask around. In larger cities, there are already groups doing this kind of thing. Check it out with one or two of your teen leaders before taking the whole group. If they are singing songs you are not familiar with, you may wish to grab the lyrics and chords and teach some of those to your group before taking them.

NEED IDEAS AND RESOURCES?

Here are some places you might want to explore to listen to more hot praise and worship music:

On the Internet

http://www.gospelcom.net/worshiptogether/
http://www.vineyardmusic.com/
http://www.integinc.com/
http://www.worshipmusic.com

In Christian Bookstores

Check out the music section. Many stores provide a listening station. Try stuff by contemporary bands Delirious?, Sonic Flood, Nitro Praise and Matt Redman, to name a few. You can also find printed songbooks and other helpful resources. God is raising up many students in this generation to truly seek him. The amount of new praise and worship music is overflowing. Who knows, maybe you have a budding songwriter in your midst. Allow your students to offer their creative talents to God and see what he can do!

Sonic
PRAISE
Rockin' Worship
for a New Generation
Date
Time
Location

Every Day in Worship

Here is what you do. Cut out the various Psalm slips and put them in a container or small box. Each day, grab a slip from the box and read it over. Try to make the following steps part of your daily discipline and worship.

1. Give yourself enough quiet, uninterrupted time to really think or meditate on what the Psalm is saying. Don't rush through it.
2. Grab a pencil or pen and underline words, phrases or verses that jump out at you as significant or inspiring.
3. Offer the Psalm back to God as an act of worship. Say it, sing it, think it.

- -

Psalm 1:1-6

"How well God must like you—you don't hang out at Sin Saloon, you don't slink along Dead-End Road, you don't go to Smart-Mouth College.

Instead you thrill to GOD's Word, you chew on Scripture day and night. You're a tree replanted in Eden, bearing fresh fruit every month, never dropping a leaf, always in blossom.

You're not at all like the wicked, who are mere windblown dust—without defense in court, unfit company for innocent people.

GOD charts the road you take. The road *they* take is Skid Row."

- -

Psalm 6:1-10

A DAVID PSALM

"Please, GOD, no more yelling, no more trips to the woodshed.

Treat me nice for a change; I'm so starved for affection.

Can't you see I'm black and blue, beat up badly in bones and soul?

GOD, how long will it take for you to let up?

Break in, GOD, and break up this fight; if you love me at all, get me out of here.

I'm no good to you dead, am I?

I can't sing in your choir if I'm buried in some tomb!

I'm tired of all this—so tired. My bed has been floating forty days and nights on the flood of my tears.

My mattress is soaked, soggy with tears.

The sockets of my eyes are black holes; nearly blind, I squint and grope.

Get out of here, you Devil's crew: at last GOD has heard my sobs.

My requests have all been granted, my prayers are answered.

Cowards, my enemies disappear.

Disgraced, they turn tail and run."

- -

Psalm 8:1-9

A DAVID PSALM

"GOD, brilliant Lord, yours is a household name.

Nursing infants gurgle choruses about you; toddlers shout the songs that drown out enemy talk, and silence atheist babble.

I look up at your macro-skies, dark and enormous, your handmade sky-jewelry, moon and stars mounted in their settings.

Then I look at my micro-self and wonder, why do you bother with us?

Why take a second look our way?

Yet we've so narrowly missed being gods, bright with Eden's dawn light.

You put us in charge of your handcrafted world, repeated to us your Genesis-charge, made us lords of sheep and cattle, even animals out in the wild, birds flying and fish swimming, whales singing in the ocean deeps.

GOD, brilliant Lord, your name echoes around the world."

- -

Psalm 15:1-5

A DAVID PSALM

"GOD, who gets invited to dinner at your place? How do we get on your guest list?

'Walk straight, act right, tell the truth. Don't hurt your friend, don't blame your neighbor; despise the despicable.

'Keep your word even when it costs you, make an honest living, never take a bribe. You'll never get blacklisted if you live like this.'"

- -

Psalm 19:1-14

A DAVID PSALM

"God's glory is on tour in the skies, God-craft on exhibit across the horizon.

Madame Day holds classes every morning, Professor Night lectures each evening.

Their words aren't heard, their voices aren't recorded, but their silence fills the earth: unspoken truth is spoken everywhere.

God makes a huge dome for the sun—a superdome! The morning sun's a new husband leaping from his honeymoon bed, the daybreaking sun an athlete racing to the tape.

That's how God's Word vaults across the skies from sunrise to sunset, melting ice, scorching deserts, warming hearts to faith.

The revelation of GOD is whole and pulls our lives together. The signposts of GOD are clear and point out the right road. The life-maps of GOD are right, showing the way to joy. The directions of GOD are plain and easy on the eyes. GOD's reputation is twenty-four carat gold, with a lifetime guarantee. The decisions of GOD are accurate down to the nth degree.

God's Word is better than a diamond, better than a diamond set between emeralds.

You'll like it better than strawberries in spring, better than red, ripe strawberries.

There's more: God's Word warns us of danger and directs us to hidden treasure. Otherwise how will we find our way? Or know when we play the fool?

Clean the slate, God, so we can start the day fresh! Keep me from stupid sins, from thinking I can take over your work; then I can start this day sun-washed, scrubbed clean of the grime of sin. These are the words in my mouth; these are what I chew on and pray. Accept them when I place them on the morning altar, O God, my Altar-Rock, God, Priest-of-My-Altar."

Psalm 23:1-6

A DAVID PSALM

"GOD, my shepherd! I don't need a thing. You have bedded me down in lush meadows, you find me quiet pools to drink from.

True to your word, you let me catch my breath and send me in the right direction. Even when the way goes through Death Valley, I'm not afraid when you walk at my side. Your trusty shepherd's crook makes me feel secure.

You serve me a six-course dinner right in front of my enemies. You revive my drooping head; my cup brims with blessing. Your beauty and love chase after me every day of my life. I'm back home in the house of GOD for the rest of my life."

Psalm 25:1-22

A DAVID PSALM

"My head is high, GOD, held high; I'm looking to you, GOD; no hangdog skulking for me. I've thrown in my lot with you; You won't embarrass me, will you? Or let my enemies get the best of me?

Don't embarrass any of us who went out on a limb for you. It's the traitors who should be humiliated.

Show me how you work, GOD; school me in your ways. Take me by the hand; lead me down the path of truth.

You are my Savior, aren't you? Mark the milestones of your mercy and love, GOD; rebuild the ancient landmarks!

Forget that I sowed wild oats; mark me with your sign of love. Plan only the best for me, GOD! GOD is fair and just; he corrects the misdirected, sends them in the right direction.

He gives the rejects his hand, and leads them step by step. From now on every road you travel will take you to GOD. Follow the Covenant signs; read the charted directions.

Keep up your reputation, GOD; forgive my bad life; it's been a very bad life.

My question: What are God-worshipers like? Your answer: Arrows aimed at God's bull's-eye. They settle down in a promising place; their kids inherit a prosperous farm. God-friendship is for God-worshipers; they are the ones he confides in.

If I keep my eyes on GOD, I won't trip over my own feet. Look at me and help me!

I'm all alone and in big trouble. My heart and kidneys are fighting each other; call a truce to this civil war. Take a hard look at my life of hard labor, then lift this ton of sin.

Do you see how many people have it in for me? How viciously they hate me? Keep watch over me and keep me out of trouble; don't let me down when I run to you. Use all your skill to put me together; I wait to see your finished product. GOD, give your people a break from this run of bad luck."

Psalm 27:1-14

A DAVID PSALM

"Light, space, zest—that's GOD! So, with him on my side I'm fearless, afraid of no one and nothing. When vandal hordes ride down ready to eat me alive, those bullies and toughs fall flat on their faces.

When besieged, I'm calm as a baby. When all hell breaks loose, I'm collected and cool. I'm asking GOD for one thing, only one thing: To live with him in his house my whole life long.

I'll contemplate his beauty; I'll study at his feet. That's the only quiet, secure place in a noisy world, the perfect getaway, far from the buzz of traffic.

God holds me head and shoulders above all who try to pull me down. I'm headed for his place to offer anthems that will raise the roof! Already I'm singing God-songs; I'm making music to GOD. Listen, GOD, I'm calling at the top of my lungs: 'Be good to me! Answer me!'

When my heart whispered, 'Seek God,' my whole being replied, 'I'm seeking him!'

Don't hide from me now! You've always been right there for me; don't turn your back on me now. Don't throw me out, don't abandon me; you've always kept the door open. My father and mother walked out and left me, but GOD took me in.

Point me down your highway, GOD; direct me along a well-lighted street; show my enemies whose side you're on. Don't throw me to the dogs, those liars who are out to get me, filling the air with their threats.

I'm sure now I'll see God's goodness in the exuberant earth. Stay with GOD! Take heart. Don't quit. I'll say it again: Stay with GOD."

Psalm 29:1-11

A David psalm

"Bravo, God, bravo! Gods and all angels shout, 'Encore!'
In awe before the glory, in awe before God's visible power. Stand at attention!
Dress your best to honor him! God thunders across the waters, brilliant, his voice and his face, streaming brightness—God, across the flood waters.
God's thunder tympanic, God's thunder symphonic. God's thunder smashes cedars, God topples the northern cedars.
The mountain ranges skip like spring colts, the high ridges jump like wild kid goats. God's thunder spits fire. God thunders, the wilderness quakes; he makes the
desert of Kadesh shake. God's thunder sets the oak trees dancing a wild dance, whirling; the pelting rain strips their branches.
We fall to our knees—we call out, 'Glory!' Above the floodwaters is God's throne from which his power flows, from which he rules the world. God makes his people
strong. God gives his people peace."

Psalm 30:1-12

A David psalm

"I give you all the credit, God—you got me out of that mess, you didn't let my foes gloat. God, my God, I yelled for help and you put me together. God, you pulled
me out of the grave, gave me another chance at life when I was down and out.
All you saints! Sing your hearts out to God! Thank him to his face! He gets angry once in a while, but across a lifetime there is only love. The nights of crying your
eyes out give way to days of laughter.
When things were going great I crowed, 'I've got it made. I'm God's favorite. He made me king of the mountain.' Then you looked the other way and I fell to pieces.
I called out to you, God; I laid my case before you: 'Can you sell me for a profit when I'm dead? auction me off at a cemetery yard sale? When I'm "dust to dust"
my songs and stories of you won't sell. So listen! and be kind! Help me out of this!'
You did it: you changed wild lament into whirling dance; you ripped off my black mourning band and decked me with wildflowers. I'm about to burst with song; I
can't keep quiet about you. God, my God, I can't thank you enough."

Psalm 32:1-11

A David psalm

"Count yourself lucky, how happy you must be—you get a fresh start, your slate's wiped clean. Count yourself lucky—God holds nothing against you and you're
holding nothing back from him.
When I kept it all inside, my bones turned to powder, my words became daylong groans. The pressure never let up; all the juices of my life dried up. Then I let it all
out; I said, 'I'll make a clean breast of my failures to God.' Suddenly the pressure was gone—my guilt dissolved, my sin disappeared.
These things add up. Every one of us needs to pray; when all hell breaks loose and the dam bursts we'll be on high ground, untouched. God's my island hideaway,
keeps danger far from the shore, throws garlands of hosannas around my neck.
Let me give you some good advice; I'm looking you in the eye and giving it to you straight: 'Don't be ornery like a horse or mule that needs bit and bridle to
stay on track.'
God-defiers are always in trouble; God-affirmers find themselves loved every time they turn around. Celebrate God. Sing together—everyone! All you honest hearts,
raise the roof!"

Psalm 34:1-22

A David psalm, when he outwitted Abimelech and got away.

"I bless God every chance I get; my lungs expand with his praise.
I live and breathe God; if things aren't going well, hear this and be happy: Join me in spreading the news; together let's get the word out.
God met me more than halfway, he freed me from my anxious fears. Look at him; give him your warmest smile. Never hide your feelings from him.
When I was desperate, I called out, and God got me out of a tight spot. God's angel sets up a circle of protection around us while we pray. Open your mouth and
taste, open your eyes and see—how good God is. Blessed are you who run to him.
Worship God if you want the best; worship opens doors to all his goodness. Young lions on the prowl get hungry, but God-seekers are full of God. Come, children,
listen closely; I'll give you a lesson in God worship.
Who out there has a lust for life? Can't wait each day to come upon beauty? Guard your tongue from profanity, and no more lying through your teeth. Turn your
back on sin; do something good. Embrace peace—don't let it get away!
God keeps an eye on his friends, his ears pick up every moan and groan. God won't put up with rebels; he'll cull them from the pack. Is anyone crying for help? God
is listening, ready to rescue you. If your heart is broken, you'll find God right there; if you're kicked in the gut, he'll help you catch your breath.
Disciples so often get into trouble; still, God is there every time. He's your bodyguard, shielding every bone; not even a finger gets broken. The wicked commit slow
suicide; they waste their lives hating the good. God pays for each slave's freedom; no one who runs to him loses out."

Psalm 42:1-11

"A white-tailed deer drinks from the creek; I want to drink God, deep draughts of God. I'm thirsty for God-alive. I wonder, 'Will I ever make it—arrive and drink in God's presence?'

I'm on a diet of tears—tears for breakfast, tears for supper. All day long people knock at my door, pestering, 'Where is this God of yours?'

These are the things I go over and over, emptying out the pockets of my life. I was always at the head of the worshiping crowd, right out in front, leading them all, eager to arrive and worship, shouting praises, singing thanksgiving—celebrating, all of us, God's feast!

Why are you down in the dumps, dear soul? Why are you crying the blues? Fix my eyes on God—soon I'll be praising again. He puts a smile on my face. He's my God.

When my soul is in the dumps, I rehearse everything I know of you, from Jordan depths to Hermon heights, including Mount Mizar. Chaos calls to chaos, to the tune of whitewater rapids. Your breaking surf, your thundering breakers crash and crush me. Then GOD promises to love me all day, sing songs all through the night!

My life is God's prayer. Sometimes I ask God, my rock-solid God, 'Why did you let me down? Why am I walking around in tears, harassed by enemies?'

They're out for the kill, these tormentors with their obscenities, taunting day after day, 'Where is this God of yours?'

Why are you down in the dumps, dear soul? Why are you crying the blues? Fix my eyes on God—soon I'll be praising again. He puts a smile on my face. He's my God."

Psalm 46:1-11

"God is a safe place to hide, ready to help when we need him. We stand fearless at the cliff-edge of doom, courageous in seastorm and earthquake, before the rush and roar of oceans, the tremors that shift mountains.

Jacob-wrestling God fights for us, GOD of angel armies protects us. River fountains splash joy, cooling God's city, this sacred haunt of the Most High. God lives here, the streets are safe, God at your service from crack of dawn.

Godless nations rant and rave, kings and kingdoms threaten, but Earth does anything he says. Jacob-wrestling God fights for us, GOD of angel armies protects us.

Attention, all! See the marvels of GOD! He plants flowers and trees all over the earth, bans war from pole to pole, breaks all the weapons across his knee.

'Step out of the traffic! Take a long, loving look at me, your High God, above politics, above everything.'

Jacob-wrestling God fights for us, GOD of angel armies protects us."

Psalm 49:1-20

"Listen, everyone, listen—earth-dwellers, don't miss this. All you haves and have-nots, all together now: listen.

I set plainspoken wisdom before you, my heart-seasoned understandings of life. I fine-tuned my ear to the sayings of the wise, I solve life's riddle with the help of a harp. So why should I fear in bad times, hemmed in by enemy malice, shoved around by bullies, demeaned by the arrogant rich?

Really! There's no such thing as self-rescue, pulling yourself up by your bootstraps. The cost of rescue is beyond our means, and even then it doesn't guarantee life forever, or insurance against the Black Hole. Anyone can see that the brightest and best die, wiped out right along with fools and dunces.

They leave all their prowess behind, move into their new home, The Coffin, the cemetery their permanent address. And to think they named counties after themselves!

We aren't immortal. We don't last long. Like our dogs, we age and weaken. And die. This is what happens to those who live for the moment, who only look out for themselves: Death herds them like sheep straight to hell; they disappear down the gullet of the grave; they waste away to nothing—nothing left but a marker in a cemetery.

But me? God snatches me from the clutch of death, he reaches down and grabs me. So don't be impressed with those who get rich and pile up fame and fortune. They can't take it with them; fame and fortune all get left behind. Just when they think they've arrived and folks praise them because they've made good, they enter the family burial plot where they'll never see sunshine again.

We aren't immortal. We don't last long. Like our dogs, we age and weaken. And die."

Psalm 51:1-19

"Generous in love—God, give grace! Huge in mercy—wipe out my bad record. Scrub away my guilt, soak out my sins in your laundry. I know how bad I've been; my sins are staring me down.

You're the One I've violated, and you've seen it all, seen the full extent of my evil. You have all the facts before you; whatever you decide about me is fair. I've been out of step with you for a long time, in the wrong since before I was born.

What you're after is truth from the inside out. Enter me, then; conceive a new, true life. Soak me in your laundry and I'll come out clean, scrub me and I'll have a snow-white life.

Tune me in to foot-tapping songs, set these once-broken bones to dancing. Don't look too close for blemishes, give me a clean bill of health. God, make a fresh start in me, shape a Genesis week from the chaos of my life. Don't throw me out with the trash, or fail to breathe holiness in me. Bring me back from gray exile, put a fresh wind in my sails!

Give me a job teaching rebels your ways so the lost can find their way home. Commute my death sentence, God, my salvation God, and I'll sing anthems to your life-giving ways. Unbutton my lips, dear God; I'll let loose with your praise.

Going through the motions doesn't please you, a flawless performance is nothing to you. I learned God-worship when my pride was shattered. Heart-shattered lives ready for love don't for a moment escape God's notice.

Make Zion the place you delight in, repair Jerusalem's broken-down walls. Then you'll get real worship from us, acts of worship small and large, including all the bulls they can heave onto your altar!"

Psalm 62:1-12

"God, the one and only—I'll wait as long as he says. Everything I need comes from him, so why not? He's solid rock under my feet, breathing room for my soul, an impregnable castle: I'm set for life.

How long will you gang up on me? How long will you run with the bullies? There's nothing to you, any of you—rotten floorboards, worm-eaten rafters, anthills plotting to bring down mountains, far gone in make-believe. You talk a good line, but every 'blessing' breathes a curse.

God, the one and only—I'll wait as long as he says. Everything I hope for comes from him, so why not? He's solid rock under my feet, breathing room for my soul, an impregnable castle: I'm set for life.

My help and glory are in God—granite-strength and safe-harbor-God—so trust him absolutely, people; lay your lives on the line for him. God is a safe place to be.

Man as such is smoke, woman as such, a mirage. Put them together, they're nothing; two times nothing is nothing. And a windfall, if it comes—don't make too much of it.

God said this once and for all; how many times have I heard it repeated? 'Strength comes straight from God.' Love to you, Lord God! You pay a fair wage for a good day's work!"

Psalm 65:1-13

"Silence is praise to you, Zion-dwelling God, and also obedience. You hear the prayer in it all. We all arrive at your doorstep sooner or later, loaded with guilt, our sins too much for us—but you get rid of them once and for all.

Blessed are the chosen! Blessed the guest at home in your place! We expect our fill of good things in your house, your heavenly manse. All your salvation wonders are on display in your trophy room. Earth-Tamer, Ocean-Pourer, Mountain-Maker, Hill-Dresser, Muzzler of sea storm and wave crash, of mobs in noisy riot—far and wide they'll come to a stop, they'll stare in awe, in wonder. Dawn and dusk take turns calling, 'Come and worship.'

Oh, visit the earth, ask her to join the dance! Deck her out in spring showers, fill the God-River with living water. Paint the wheat fields golden. Creation was made for this! Drench the plowed fields, soak the dirt clods with rainfall as harrow and rake bring her to blossom and fruit. Snow-crown the peaks with splendor, scatter rose petals down your paths, all through the wild meadows, rose petals.

Set the hills to dancing, dress the canyon walls with live sheep, a drape of flax across the valleys. Let them shout, and shout, and shout! Oh, oh, let them sing!"

Psalm 77:1-20

"I yell out to my God, I yell with all my might, I yell at the top of my lungs. He listens. I found myself in trouble and went looking for my Lord; my life was an open wound that wouldn't heal. When friends said, 'Everything will turn out all right,' I didn't believe a word they said.

I remember God—and shake my head. I bow my head—then wring my hands. I'm awake all night—not a wink of sleep; I can't even say what's bothering me. I go over the days one by one, I ponder the years gone by. I strum my lute all through the night, wondering how to get my life together.

Will the Lord walk off and leave us for good? Will he never smile again? Is his love worn threadbare? Has his salvation promise burned out? Has God forgotten his manners? Has he angrily stalked off and left us? 'Just my luck,' I said. 'The High God goes out of business just the moment I need him.'

Once again I'll go over what GOD has done, lay out on the table the ancient wonders; I'll ponder all the things you've accomplished, and give a long, loving look at your acts. Oh God! Your way is holy! No god is great like God! You're the God who makes things happen; you showed everyone what you can do—you pulled your people out of the worst kind of trouble, rescued the children of Jacob and Joseph.

Ocean saw you in action, God, saw you and trembled with fear; Deep Ocean was scared to death. Clouds belched buckets of rain, Sky exploded with thunder, your arrows flashing this way and that. From Whirlwind came your thundering voice, Lightning exposed the world, Earth reeled and rocked.

You strode right through Ocean, walked straight through roaring Ocean, but nobody saw you come or go. Hidden in the hands of Moses and Aaron, you led your people like a flock of sheep."

Psalm 84:1-12

"What a beautiful home, GOD of the Angel Armies! I've always longed to live in a place like this, always dreamed of a room in your house, where I could sing for joy to God-alive!

Birds find nooks and crannies in your house, sparrows and swallows make nests there. They lay their eggs and raise their young, singing their songs in the place where we worship. GOD of the Angel Armies! King! God! How blessed they are to live and sing there!

And how blessed all those in whom you live, whose lives become roads you travel; they wind through lonesome valleys, come upon brooks, discover cool springs and pools brimming with rain! God-traveled, these roads curve up the mountain, and at the last turn—Zion! God in full view!

God of the Angel Armies, listen: O God of Jacob, open your ears—I'm praying! Look at our shields, glistening in the sun, our faces, shining with your gracious anointing.

One day spent in your house, this beautiful place of worship, beats thousands spent on Greek island beaches. I'd rather scrub floors in the house of my God than be honored as a guest in the palace of sin.

All sunshine and sovereign is GOD, generous in gifts and glory. He doesn't scrimp with his traveling companions. It's smooth sailing all the way with GOD of the Angel Armies."

Psalm 92:1-15

"What a beautiful thing, God, to give thanks, to sing an anthem to you, the High God! To announce your love each daybreak, sing your faithful presence all through the night, accompanied by dulcimer and harp, the full-bodied music of strings.

You made me so happy, God. I saw your work and I shouted for joy. How magnificent your work, God! How profound your thoughts!

Dullards never notice what you do; fools never do get it. When the wicked popped up like weeds and all the evil men and women took over, you mowed them down, finished them off once and for all. You, God, are High and Eternal. Look at your enemies, God! Look at your enemies—ruined! Scattered to the winds, all those hirelings of evil!

But you've made me strong as a charging bison, you've honored me with a festive parade. The sight of my critics going down is still fresh, the rout of my malicious detractors. My ears are filled with the sounds of promise: 'Good people will prosper like palm trees, grow tall like Lebanon cedars; transplanted to God's courtyard, they'll grow tall in the presence of God, lithe and green, virile still in old age.'

Such witnesses to upright God! My Mountain, my huge, holy Mountain!"

Psalm 93:1-5

"God is King, robed and ruling, God is robed and surging with strength. And yes, the world is firm, immovable, your throne ever firm—you're Eternal!

Sea storms are up, God, sea storms wild and roaring, sea storms with thunderous breakers. Stronger than wild sea storms, mightier than sea-storm breakers, Mighty God rules from High Heaven.

What you say goes—it always has. 'Beauty' and 'Holy' mark your palace rule, God, to the very end of time."

Psalm 95:1-11

"Come, let's shout praises to God, raise the roof for the Rock who saved us! Let's march into his presence singing praises, lifting the rafters with our hymns!

And why? Because God is the best, High King over all the gods. In one hand he holds deep caves and caverns, in the other hand grasps the high mountains. He made Ocean—he owns it! His hands sculpted Earth!

So come, let us worship: bow before him, on your knees before God, who made us! Oh yes, he's our God, and we're the people he pastures, the flock he feeds.

Drop everything and listen, listen as he speaks: 'Don't turn a deaf ear as in the Bitter Uprising, as on the day of the Wilderness Test, when your ancestors turned and put *me* to the test. For forty years they watched me at work among them, as over and over they tried my patience. And I was provoked—oh, was I provoked!

"Can't they keep their minds on God for five minutes? Do they simply refuse to walk down my road?" Exasperated, I exploded, "They'll never get where they're headed, never be able to sit down and rest."'"

Psalm 96:1-13

"Sing God a brand-new song! Earth and everyone in it, sing! Sing to God—*worship* God! Shout the news of his victory from sea to sea, take the news of his glory to the lost, news of his wonders to one and all!

For God is great, and worth a thousand Hallelujahs. His terrible beauty makes the gods look cheap; pagan gods are mere tatters and rags. God made the heavens—royal splendor radiates from him, a powerful beauty sets him apart.

Bravo, God, Bravo! Everyone join in the great shout: Encore! In awe before the beauty, in awe before the might. Bring gifts and celebrate, bow before the beauty of God, then to your knees—everyone worship!

Get out the message—God Rules! He put the world on a firm foundation; he treats everyone fair and square. Let's hear it from Sky, with Earth joining in, and a huge round of applause from Sea.

Let Wilderness turn cartwheels, animals, come dance, put every tree of the forest in the choir—an extravaganza before God as he comes, as he comes to set everything right on earth, set everything right, treat everyone fair."

Psalm 97:1-12

"God rules: *there's* something to shout over! On the double, mainlands and islands—celebrate! Bright clouds and storm clouds circle 'round him; right and justice anchor his rule.

Fire blazes out before him, flaming high up the craggy mountains. His lightnings light up the world; Earth, wide-eyed, trembles in fear.

The mountains take one look at God and melt, melt like wax before earth's Lord. The heavens announce that he'll set everything right, and everyone will see it happen—glorious!

All who serve handcrafted gods will be sorry—and they were so proud of their ragamuffin gods! On your knees, all you gods—worship him! And Zion, you listen and take heart!

Daughters of Zion, sing your hearts out: God has done it all, has set everything right. You, God, are High God of the cosmos, far, far higher than any of the gods.

God loves all who hate evil, and those who love him he keeps safe, snatches them from the grip of the wicked.

Light-seeds are planted in the souls of God's people, joy-seeds are planted in good heart-soil. So, God's people, shout praise to God, give thanks to our Holy God!"

Psalm 98:1-9

"Sing to God a brand-new song. He's made a world of wonders! He rolled up his sleeves, He set things right. God made history with salvation, He showed the world what he could do. He remembered to love us, a bonus to his dear family, Israel—indefatigable love.

The whole earth comes to attention. Look—God's work of salvation. Shout your praises to God, everybody! Let loose and sing! Strike up the band! Round up an orchestra to play for God, add on a hundred-voice choir. Feature trumpets and big trombones, fill the air with praises to King God.

Let the sea and its fish give a round of applause, with everything living on earth joining in. Let ocean breakers call out, 'Encore!' And mountains harmonize the finale—a tribute to God when he comes, when he comes to set the earth right. He'll straighten out the whole world, he'll put the world right, and everyone in it."

Psalm 103:1-22

"Oh my soul, bless GOD. From head to toe, I'll bless his holy name! Oh my soul, bless GOD, don't forget a single blessing!

He forgives your sins—every one. He heals your diseases—every one. He redeems you from hell—saves your life! He crowns you with love and mercy—a paradise crown. He wraps you in goodness—beauty eternal. He renews your youth—you're always young in his presence.

GOD makes everything come out right; he puts victims back on their feet. He showed Moses how he went about his work, opened up his plans to all Israel.

GOD is sheer mercy and grace; not easily angered, he's rich in love. He doesn't endlessly nag and scold, nor hold grudges forever. He doesn't treat us as our sins deserve, nor pay us back in full for our wrongs.

As high as heaven is over the earth, so strong is his love to those who fear him. And as far as sunrise is from sunset, he has separated us from our sins.

As parents feel for their children, GOD feels for those who fear him. He knows us inside and out, keeps in mind that we're made of mud. Men and women don't live very long; like wildflowers they spring up and blossom, But a storm snuffs them out just as quickly, leaving nothing to show they were here.

GOD's love, though, is ever and always, eternally present to all who fear him, making everything right for them and their children as they follow his Covenant ways and remember to do whatever he said. GOD has set his throne in heaven; he rules over us all. He's the King!

So bless GOD, you angels, ready and able to fly at his bidding, quick to hear and do what he says. Bless GOD, all you armies of angels, alert to respond to whatever he wills. Bless GOD, all creatures, wherever you are—everything and everyone made by GOD. And you, oh my soul, bless GOD!"

Psalm 111:1-10

"Hallelujah! I give thanks to GOD with everything I've got—wherever good people gather, and in the congregation.

GOD's works are so great, worth a lifetime of study—endless enjoyment! Splendor and beauty mark his craft; his generosity never gives out. His miracles are his memorial—this GOD of Grace, this GOD of Love.

He gave food to those who fear him, he remembered to keep his ancient promise. He proved to his people that he could do what he said: Hand them the nations on a platter—a gift!

He manufactures truth and justice; all his products are guaranteed to last—never out-of-date, never obsolete, rust-proof. All that he makes and does is honest and true: He paid the ransom for his people, he ordered his Covenant kept forever.

He's so personal and holy, worthy of our respect. The good life begins in the fear of GOD—do that and you'll know the blessing of GOD. His Hallelujah lasts forever!"

Psalm 113:1-9

"Hallelujah! You who serve GOD, praise GOD! Just to speak his name is praise! Just to remember GOD is a blessing—now and tomorrow and always. From east to west, from dawn to dusk, keep lifting all your praises to GOD!

GOD is higher than anything and anyone, outshining everything you can see in the skies. Who can compare with GOD, our God, so majestically enthroned, surveying his magnificent heavens and earth?

He picks up the poor from out of the dirt, rescues the wretched who've been thrown out with the trash, seats them among the honored guests, a place of honor among the brightest and best. He gives childless couples a family, gives them joy as the parents of children. Hallelujah!"

Psalm 121:1-8

"I look up to the mountains; does my strength come from mountains? No, my strength comes from GOD, who made heaven, and earth, and mountains.

He won't let you stumble, your Guardian God won't fall asleep. Not on your life! Israel's Guardian will never doze or sleep.

GOD's your Guardian, right at your side to protect you—shielding you from sunstroke, sheltering you from moonstroke.

GOD guards you from every evil, he guards your very life. He guards you when you leave and when you return, he guards you now, he guards you always."

Psalm 125:1-5

"Those who trust in GOD are like Zion Mountain: nothing can move it, a rock-solid mountain you can always depend on. Mountains encircle Jerusalem, and GOD encircles his people—always has and always will.

The fist of the wicked will never violate what is due the righteous, provoking wrongful violence. Be good to your good people, GOD, to those whose hearts are right! GOD will round up the backsliders, corral them with the incorrigibles. Peace over Israel!"

Psalm 133:1-3

"How wonderful, how beautiful, when brothers and sisters get along! It's like costly anointing oil flowing down head and beard, flowing down Aaron's beard, flowing down the collar of his priestly robes. It's like the dew on Mount Hermon flowing down the slopes of Zion. Yes, that's where GOD commands the blessing, ordains eternal life."

Psalm 136:1-26

"Thank God! He deserves your thanks. *His love never quits.* Thank the God of all gods, *His love never quits.* Thank the Lord of all lords. *His love never quits.*

Thank the miracle-working God, *His love never quits.* The God whose skill formed the cosmos, *His love never quits.* The God who laid out earth on ocean foundations, *His love never quits.*

The God who filled the skies with light, *His love never quits.* The sun to watch over the day, *His love never quits.* Moon and stars as guardians of the night, *His love never quits.*

The God who struck down the Egyptian firstborn, *His love never quits.* And rescued Israel from Egypt's oppression, *His love never quits.* Took Israel in hand with his powerful hand, *His love never quits.*

Split the Red Sea right in half, *His love never quits.* Led Israel right through the middle, *His love never quits.* Dumped Pharaoh and his army in the sea, *His love never quits.*

The God who marched his people through the desert, *His love never quits.* Smashed huge kingdoms right and left, *His love never quits.* Struck down the famous kings, *His love never quits.*

Struck Sihon the Amorite king, *His love never quits.* Struck Og the Bashanite king, *His love never quits.* Then distributed their land as booty, *His love never quits.*

Handed the land over to Israel. *His love never quits.* God remembered us when we were down, *His love never quits.* Rescued us from the trampling boot, *His love never quits.*

Takes care of everyone in time of need. *His love never quits.* Thank God, who did it all! *His love never quits.*"

Psalm 146:1-10

"Hallelujah! Oh my soul, praise God! All my life long I'll praise God, singing songs to my God as long as I live.

Don't put your life in the hands of experts who know nothing of life, of *salvation* life. Mere humans don't have what it takes; when they die, their projects die with them. Instead, get help from the God of Jacob, put your hope in God and know real blessing! God made sky and soil, sea and all the fish in it.

He always does what he says—he defends the wronged, he feeds the hungry. God frees prisoners—he gives sight to the blind, he lifts up the fallen. God loves good people, protects strangers, takes the side of orphans and widows, but makes short work of the wicked.

God's in charge—*always.* Zion's God is God for good! Hallelujah!"

Psalm 148:1-14

"Hallelujah! Praise God from heaven, praise him from the mountaintops; praise him, all you his angels, praise him, all you his warriors, praise him, sun and moon, praise him, you morning stars; praise him, high heaven, praise him, heavenly rain clouds; praise, oh let them praise the name of God—he spoke the word, and there they were!

He set them in place from all time to eternity; he gave his orders, and that's it!

Praise God from earth, you sea dragons, you fathomless ocean deeps; fire and hail, snow and ice, hurricanes obeying his orders; mountains and all hills, apple orchards and cedar forests; wild beasts and herds of cattle, snakes, and birds in flight; Earth's kings and all races, leaders and important people, robust men and women in their prime, and yes, graybeards and little children.

Let them praise the name of God—it's the only Name worth praising. His radiance exceeds anything in earth and sky; he's built a monument—his very own people! Praise from all who love God! Israel's children, intimate friends of God. Hallelujah!"

Psalm 150:1-6

"Hallelujah! Praise God in his holy house of worship, praise him under the open skies; praise him for his acts of power, praise him for his magnificent greatness; praise with a blast on the trumpet, praise by strumming soft strings; praise him with castanets and dance, praise him with banjo and flute; praise him with cymbals and a big bass drum, praise him with fiddles and mandolin.

Let every living, breathing creature praise God! Hallelujah!"

Song Chords

"Everything I Want (Is in You)"

Words and music by Spooky Tuesday
© 1999 This donkey saw an angel (BMI)

[CHORUS]:

```
A             D   E         A
The name of the Lord is all that I need.

A/C#       D   E        A
The words of the Father is all I want to speak.
```

[VERSE]:

```
A
Everything I want is in You,

D
And I will never need the world.

A
Everything I want comes from You,

D
All of my desires are fulfilled.

A
Everything I want is in You,

D
And I will never need the world.

A
Everything I want comes from You,

D
All of my desires are fulfilled.
```

[BRIDGE]:

```
D                          E
So with my hands I'm gonna serve You,

A                     D
With my mouth I'm gonna speak Your truth.
```

```
D                    E
With my life I'm gonna worship,

              D
I'm gonna take Your love and give it to the

E
world,

   E
Gonna give it to the world.
```

[CHORUS]:

```
A             D   E        A
The name of the Lord is all that I need.

A             D   E            A A/C# D E
The words of the Father is all I want to speak,

              A
Is all I want to speak.
```

[VERSE]

[BRIDGE]

[CHORUS]:

```
   A        D   E      A
The name of the Lord is all that I need.

A           D   E          A
The words of the Father is all I want to speak,

            D   E        A
The name of the Lord is all that I need.

A           D   E            A
The words of the Father is all I want to speak.
```

"Psalm 130"

Music © 1999 Thirsty moon river publishing (ASCAP)

[VERSE]:

```
G          D  Bm        C  D
Out of the depths I cry to You, O Lord.

G              D
Lord, hear my voice,

        Bm      C   D     G
Let Your ears be attentive to my cry

G   D   Bm  C D GD  Bm   C  D
For mercy, for mercy, for mercy.

    G    D        Bm      C D
If You, O Lord, kept a record of sins,

   G          D
Lord, who could stand?

      Bm            C   D
But with You there is forgiveness

      G         D    Bm     C  D
Therefore You are feared, You are feared,

G   D  Bm C  D
You are feared.
```

[CHORUS]:

```
    Em                D
Praise the Lord, all you nations extol Him,

    Em            D
All you peoples, for great is His love toward

G
us.

   G     D         C        C/D
The faithfulness of the Lord endures forever,

G       D C C/D G  D   C C/D C D
Praise the Lord, praise the Lord.
```

[VERSE 2]:

```
   G            D
I wait for the Lord

       Bm          C  D
And in His Word I put my hope.

   G         D      Bm C D
My soul waits for the Lord

    G           D      Bm           C  D
More than watchmen wait for the morning,

G    D   Bm  C D
I wait for the Lord.

       GD   Bm      C      D
O Israel, put your hope in the Lord,

    G         D       Bm
For with the Lord is unfailing love

    C          D
And full redemption.

G    D      Bm   C    D  G
He Himself will redeem Israel

G    D      Bm  C D
From all their sins.
```

[CHORUS]:

```
    Em                D
Praise the Lord, all you nations extol Him,

       Em           D            G
All you peoples, for great is His love toward us.

   G     D         C        C/D
The faithfulness of the Lord endures forever,

G       D C C/D G  D   C C/D
Praise the Lord, praise the Lord,

G       D C C/D C D G
Praise the Lord.
```

"All Lids (Psalm 63)"

Words and music by Soul-Junk
© 1999 Galaxy control music (ASCAP)

[VERSE 1]:

```
E                   B   E
O God, You are my God,

E               B   E
Earnestly I seek You.

E                 B   E
My soul thirsts for You,

E                     B     E
And my body longs for You.
```

[CHORUS]:

```
E           B/G#        A
Find rest, my soul, in God alone.

A
(My hope comes from Him, my hope comes

        E
from Him.)

E           B/G#        A
Find rest, my soul, in God alone.

A
(He alone is my rock and my salvation.)

E           B/G#        A
Find rest, my soul, in God alone.
```

[VERSE 2]:

```
E                       B   E
I have seen You in the sanctuary,

E                          B   E
Beheld Your power and Your glory,

E                         B    E
Because Your love is better than life,

E                    B   E
And my lips will glorify You.
```

[CHORUS]:

```
E           B/G#        A
Find rest, my soul, in God alone.

A
(My hope comes from Him, my hope comes

        E
from Him.)

E           B/G#        A
Find rest, my soul, in God alone.

A
(He alone is my rock and my salvation.)

E           B/G#        A
Find rest, my soul, in God alone.

A
(He is my fortress, I won't be shaken.)

E           B/G#        A
Find rest, my soul, in God alone.
```

[VERSE 3]:

```
E                       B    E
I will praise You as long as I live,

E                          B       E
And in Your name I will lift up my hands,

E                        B    E
You satisfy me like the richest food,

E                            B      E
With singing lips my mouth will praise You.
```

[FIRST CHORUS]

[VERSE 1]

[SECOND CHORUS]

"Just a Closer Walk With Thee"

Traditional, performed by Havalina Rail Co.

[REFRAIN]:

```
C                        G
Just a closer walk with Thee,

G                     C
Grant it, Jesus, is my plea,

C                          F
Daily walking close to Thee,

      C      G      C
Let it be, dear Lord, let it be.
```

[VERSE 1]:

```
C                        G
I am weak but Thou art strong,

G                       C
Jesus, keep me from all wrong.

C                F
I'll be satisfied as long

      C      G           C
As I walk, let me walk close to Thee.
```

[REFRAIN]:

```
C                        G
Just a closer walk with Thee,

G                     C
Grant it, Jesus, is my plea,

C                          F
Daily walking close to Thee,

      C      G      C
Let it be, dear Lord, let it be.
```

[VERSE 2]:

```
C                          G
Thro' this world of toil and snares

G                     C
If I falter, Lord, who cares?
```

```
C                              F
Who with me my burden shares?

            C       G          C
None but Thee, dear Lord, none but Thee.
```

[REFRAIN]:

```
C                        G
Just a closer walk with Thee,

G                     C
Grant it, Jesus, is my plea,

C                          F
Daily walking close to Thee,

      C      G      C
Let it be, dear Lord, let it be.
```

[VERSE 3]:

```
C                        G
When my feeble life is done,

G                     C
Time for me will be no more;

C                          F
Guide me safely to that shore,

      C      G      C
Let it be, dear Lord, let it be.
```

[REFRAIN]

"A Brighter Way"

Words and music by Sierra Hart
© 1999 High art for the working class (ASCAP)

[CHORUS]:

```
D              A       G       D
Thank You for coming into my world,

D              A          G       D
Thank You for giving me the light of day.

D              A       G       D
Thank You for coming into my world,

D              A          G       D
Thank You for showing me a brighter way.
```

[VERSE 1]:

```
A               C              G
Thank You for giving me Your Son,

A               C                G
Thank You for when Your mercies come,

A               C
Thank You for showing me

             G
You're the One who could save me.
```

[CHORUS]:

```
D              A       G       D
Thank You for coming into my world,

D              A          G       D
Thank You for giving me the light of day.

D              A       G       D
Thank You for coming into my world,

D              A          G       D
Thank You for showing me a brighter way.
```

[VERSE 2]:

```
A                          C          G
Thank You that You're faithful when I stray,

A               C                    G
Thank You for the price You were willing to pay,
```

```
A                    C
Thank You that You've promised

                  G
You'll always stay close beside me.
```

[CHORUS]:

```
D              A       G       D
Thank You for coming into my world,

D              A          G       D
Thank You for giving me the light of day.

D              A       G       D
Thank You for coming into my world,

D              A          G       D
Thank You for showing me a brighter way.
```

[BRIDGE]:

```
E                A          D
You're the truest love I'll ever know,

E                A          D
You're the truest love I'll ever know,

E                A          D
You're the truest love I'll ever know.
```

[CHORUS]:

```
D              A       G       D
Thank You for coming into my world,

D              A          G       D
Thank You for giving me the light of day.

D              A       G       D
Thank You for coming into my world,

D              A          G       D
Thank You for showing me a brighter way.
```

"Offered Myself"

Words and music by Spooky Tuesday
© 1999 This donkey saw an angel (BMI)

[VERSE]:

```
         E              C#m
When You come the whole world will

              B
know Your name

          E                      C#m
And the truth will be heard and burn purer

         B
than a flame.

          E                   C#m
I will dance unto You as You bring me to

    B
Yourself.

          E                      C#m
I will sing of Your love as I have offered

   B         E
myself to You.
```

[CHORUS]:

```
  E            F#m         A
Lord, make me pure, help me be who You

  B
desire,

  E            F#m            A
Make my heart whole, it's Your peace that I

  B
desire.

C#m                      A
Stay with me as I have offered myself,

C#m                      A
Set me free, I shall no longer be hidden.

C#m                       A      B   E
I will be true as I have offered myself to You.
```

[VERSE]:

```
         E              C#m
When You come the whole world will

              B
know Your name

          E                      C#m
And the truth will be heard and burn purer

         B
than a flame.

              E                    C#m
And I will dance unto You as You bring me

          B
to Yourself.

          E                      C#m
I will sing of Your love as I have offered

   B         E
myself to You.
```

[CHORUS]:

```
  E            F#m         A
Lord, make me pure, help me be who You

   B
desire,

  E             F#m              A
Make my heart whole, it's Your peace that I

   B
desire.

C#m                      A
Stay with me as I have offered myself,

C#m                        A
Set me free, I shall no longer be hidden.

C#m                          A       B    E
I will be true as I have offered myself to You.
```

"Everything I Want (Is in You)"
Words and music by Spooky Tuesday
© 1999 This donkey saw an angel (BMI)

[CHORUS]:
The name of the Lord is all that I need.
The words of the Father is all I want to speak.

[VERSE]:
Everything I want is in You,
And I will never need the world.
Everything I want comes from You,
All of my desires are fulfilled.
Everything I want is in You,
And I will never need the world.
Everything I want comes from You,
All of my desires are fulfilled.

[BRIDGE]:
So with my hands I'm gonna serve You,
With my mouth I'm gonna speak Your truth.
With my life I'm gonna worship,
I'm gonna take Your love and give it to the world,
Gonna give it to the world.

Everything I have is in You,
You're everything I need.

"Psalm 130"
Music © 1999 Thirsty moon river publishing (ASCAP)

[VERSE 1]:
Out of the depths I cry to You, O Lord.
Lord, hear my voice,
Let Your ears be attentive to my cry
For mercy, for mercy, for mercy.

If You, O Lord, kept a record of sins,
Lord, who could stand?
But with You there is forgiveness;
Therefore You are feared, You are feared, You are
feared.

[CHORUS]:
Praise the Lord, all you nations extol Him,
All you peoples, for great is His love toward us.
The faithfulness of the Lord endures forever,
Praise the Lord, praise the Lord.

[VERSE 2]:
I wait for the Lord
And in His Word I put my hope.
My soul waits for the Lord
More than watchmen wait for the morning,
I wait for the Lord.

O Israel, put your hope in the Lord,
For with the Lord is unfailing love
And full redemption.
He Himself will redeem Israel
From all their sins.

[CHORUS]

"All Lids (Psalm 63)"
Words and music by Soul-Junk
© 1999 Galaxy control music (ASCAP)

[VERSE 1]:
O God, You are my God,
Earnestly I seek You.
My soul thirsts for You,
And my body longs for You.

[CHORUS]:
Find rest, my soul, in God alone.
(My hope comes from Him, my hope comes from
Him.)
Find rest, my soul, in God alone.
(He alone is my rock and my salvation.)
Find rest, my soul, in God alone.

[VERSE 2]:
I have seen You in the sanctuary,
Beheld Your power and Your glory,
Because Your love is better than life,
And my lips will glorify You.

[CHORUS]:
Find rest, my soul, in God alone.
(My hope comes from Him, my hope comes from
Him.)
Find rest, my soul, in God alone.
(He alone is my rock and my salvation.)
Find rest, my soul, in God alone.
(He is my fortress, I won't be shaken.)
Find rest, my soul, in God alone.

[VERSE 3]:
I will praise You as long as I live,
And in Your name I will lift up my hands,
You satisfy me like the richest food,
With singing lips my mouth will praise You.

[CHORUS]

"Just a Closer Walk With Thee"
Traditional, performed by Havalina Rail Co.

[REFRAIN]:
Just a closer walk with Thee,
Grant it, Jesus, is my plea,
Daily walking close to Thee,
Let it be, dear Lord, let it be.

[VERSE 1]:
I am weak but Thou art strong,
Jesus, keep me from all wrong.
I'll be satisfied as long
As I walk, let me walk close to Thee.

[REFRAIN]

[VERSE 2]:
Thro' this world of toil and snares
If I falter, Lord, who cares?
Who with me my burden shares?
None but Thee, dear Lord, none but Thee.

[REFRAIN]

[VERSE 3]:
When my feeble life is o'er,
Time for me will be no more;
Guide me gently, safely o'er to Thy kingdom shore,
To Thy shore.

[REFRAIN]

"A Brighter Way"

Words and music by Sierra Hart
© 1999 High art for the working class (ASCAP)

[CHORUS]:
Thank You for coming into my world,
Thank You for giving me the light of day.
Thank You for coming into my world,
Thank You for showing me a brighter way.

[VERSE 1]:
Thank You for giving me Your Son,
Thank You for when Your mercies come,
Thank You for showing me
You're the One who could save me.

[CHORUS]

[VERSE 2]:
Thank You that You're faithful when I stray,
Thank You for the price You were willing to pay,
Thank You that You've promised
You'll always stay close beside me.

[CHORUS]

[BRIDGE]:
You're the truest love I'll ever know,
You're the truest love I'll ever know,
You're the truest love I'll ever know.

[CHORUS]

"Offered Myself"

Words and music by Spooky Tuesday
© 1999 This donkey saw an angel (BMI)

[VERSE]:
When You come the whole world will know Your
	name
And the truth will be heard and burn purer than a
	flame.
I will dance unto You as You bring me to Yourself.
I will sing of Your love as I have offered myself to
	You.

[CHORUS]:
Lord, make me pure, help me be who You desire,
Make my heart whole, it's Your peace that I desire.
Stay with me as I have offered myself,
Set me free, I shall no longer be hidden.
I will be true as I have offered myself to You.

Other EMPOWERED™ YOUTH PRODUCTS from Standard Publishing

SOME KIND OF JOURNEY ON THE ROAD WITH AUDIO ADRENALINE

Jim Burgen, Ginny McCabe and Dale Reeves

Seven strangers from across the country spent a week on the road with one of today's hottest Christian bands, Audio Adrenaline. Why? To talk about seven relevant issues that concern today's youth—such as depression, sex, prejudice and divorce. Includes an AudioVision CD with interactive discussions, songs, videos and more! You'll also get behind-the-scenes tour photos of the band and the seven people who journeyed with them.

order # 03304
(ISBN 0-7847-0744-8)

SOME KIND OF JOURNEY ON THE ROAD WITH AUDIO ADRENALINE

VIDEO CURRICULUM

This innovative video curriculum is divided into seven segments perfect for youth group discussion. Included with the 90-minute video is a leader's guide to help you challenge your teens to grapple with the same issues that are discussed on the video—things like absolutes, swearing, homosexuality. Also included is a coupon good for $2.00 off any number of copies of the companion book, SOME KIND OF JOURNEY: ON THE ROAD WITH AUDIO ADRENALINE.

order # 03318
(UPC 7-07529-03318-1)

MORE POWER TO YA THE PETRA DEVOTIONAL

Bob Hartman

Known for their biblically-based lyrics and an uncompromising stand for Christ, Petra has sold more than six million recordings and received three Grammy awards and numerous Dove awards. Bob Hartman, founding member of Petra, reveals the Scriptures, stories and personal anecdotes behind 52 of Petra's megahits in this spiral-bound devotional. This one-of-a-kind collector's item features lyrics, full-color art of all of Petra's album covers, eight pages of scrapbook photos, biographical information, a chronological history of the band's 25-year history and a Scripture and song index.

order # 03305
(ISBN 0-7847-0615-8)

REBECCA ST. JAMES 40 DAYS WITH GOD

A DEVOTIONAL JOURNAL

Australian recording artist Rebecca St. James shares her personal walk with God in this inspiring devotional book. This spiral-bound journal features sections from Rebecca's personal journal, lyric excerpts from her songs, Scripture passages and space for you to record your own thoughts. Also included are eight pages of full-color scrapbook photos and a bonus CD-ROM with three music videos, five songs and several interviews with Rebecca.

order # 03303
(ISBN 0-7847-0569-0)

TO ORDER, CONTACT YOUR LOCAL CHRISTIAN BOOKSTORE.

(IF THE BOOK IS OUT OF STOCK, YOU CAN ORDER BY CALLING 1-800-543-1353.)